THE
ARCHER-SHEES AGAINST THE
ADMIRALTY
The Story Behind *The Winslow Boy*

THE ARCHER-SHEES AGAINST THE ADMIRALTY

THE STORY BEHIND *THE WINSLOW BOY*

RODNEY M. BENNETT

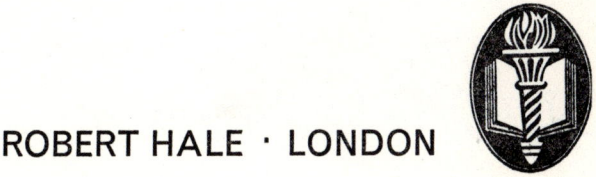

ROBERT HALE · LONDON

ISBN 0 7091 3676 5

Robert Hale & Company
63 Old Brompton Road
London SW 7

Printed in Great Britain by A. Wheaton & Co., Exeter

CONTENTS

ILLUSTRATIONS

7

PREFACE

The story told in this book is best known through Sir Terence Rattigan's play *The Winslow Boy*; however, as Sir Terence readily acknowledges, though his play was inspired by the Archer-Shee case the characters in it are largely drawn from the author's imagination and the facts altered to suit dramatic needs. The true story has been recounted briefly on a number of occasions, most notably by the American essayist Alexander Woollcott; various biographies of Sir Edward Carson and Sir Rufus Isaacs have also devoted a chapter to it.

The full story is well worth telling in detail, particularly as the Admiralty papers and other important documents have now become available. It is also valuable to place the events against the political and naval background of the period and to bring out the religious aspects. The official papers were carefully guarded during the fifty years before they were released to the Public Record Office, and I have been told of two occasions since the Second World War when requests to examine them were refused; however today I have received every co-operation from almost everyone who could assist at either the official or unofficial level.

Footnotes in the text of the book indicate selected key sources, particularly where these are new and especially interesting, and the second appendix contains details of my sources. I have avoided endeavouring to pin each source down as it occurs, for this would have become very repetitious as one Public Record file has been the source of a substantial quantity of my information. However I trust serious scholars will have no difficulty in tracing any reference they wish to follow through.

I have to thank members of the Archer-Shee family, including Lieutenant-Colonel and Mrs Jack Archer-Shee, Major and Mrs Robert Archer-Shee, the late Sister Winifrede Archer-Shee and Miss Mary

Archer-Shee, whose help has been invaluable. However, I should like to make it clear that the book was not written at their instigation or request and the final manuscript was not submitted to any of them for approval.

Those who were at Osborne during these events with whom I have made contact are Mr G. B. Smith, an English teacher from 1904–1916; five members of 'Drake' term with George Archer-Shee in 1908: Captains C. A. Kershaw and C. M. Butlin ('Beaky' and 'The Butler' of page 44), Colonel Sir Hugh Bousted, Captains D. C. Morrison and, A. H. Parsons. I have also had help from T. G. Bedwell, who was at Osborne in 1909 and who has been responsible for the preservation of some records; the widow of the late Rear-Admiral (E) D. P. Foster; W. P. Chambers and Rear-Admiral Sir Matthew Slattery. Other valuable contemporary recollections have come from Mr Percy Evans, Assistant Postmaster at Nailsworth in 1910, and Mrs Elene Boucher, a friend of the Archer-Shee family.

I have also received useful help from Mr David McKenna, the Hon Edward Carson, the Earl of Cromer, Father Godfrey Anstruther OP, the Secretary of the Bank of England, and by no means least the Headmaster of Stonyhurst College, Father G. H. Earle, SJ, and members of his staff.

Libraries and other institutions which have provided material and whose staff have always been most willing to assist include the Public Record Office; Churchill College, Cambridge; the Post Office Records Dapartments—where I am particularly grateful to Mrs C. McNamara for digging out the original postal orders; the Ministry of Defence (Navy) Library and Rear-Admiral Buckley of the Naval Historical Department; Dartmouth Naval College; Osborne House; the British Museum Library; the Finsbury Library; and the Public Libraries of the City of Westminster and the Royal Borough of Kensington and Chelsea.

Finally to my father, Captain Geoffrey Bennett, DSC RN, a well-established naval historian, I owe both the original inspiration and much good advice, and to Mr H. Montgomery Hyde, whose own writings include an authoritative biography of Sir Edward Carson, I am particularly indebted for reading through the manuscript and making invaluable comments.

London   RODNEY M. BENNETT
January, 1972

1

OSBORNE AND THE EDWARDIAN NAVY

They delivered letters on Sundays in those days. It was a letter which arrived at the home of the Bank of England's West Country Agent in Bristol on Sunday 18th October 1908 that gave Mr Archer-Shee the first knowledge of the troubles of his youngest son George; it was also to start of one of the most determined and bravest struggles of an individual against obstinate bureaucracy in British History.

The letter came from the Secretary of the Admiralty. Mr Archer-Shee's connection with the Royal Navy at the time was that George had recently started training to make his career as a naval officer. At the beginning of the year the 13-year-old boy had proudly and hopefully joined Osborne College on the Isle of Wight, which was then the starting point for young gentlemen with such aspirations. He had completed two terms and recently returned for his third; he seemed to be doing well enough even if it had been reported that not all his classroom work was up to the mark—still, a little extra effort should be able to cure this.

The letter bitterly hurt his family and ended all his own hopes.

Confidential

N.--11108

Admiralty
17th October 1908

Sir,

I am commanded by my Lords Commissioners of the Admiralty to inform you that they have received a letter from the Commanding Officer of the Royal Naval College at Osborne reporting the theft of a postal order at the College on the 7th instant which was afterwards cashed at the Post Office.

Investigation of the circumstances of the case leaves no other conclusion possible than that the postal order was taken by your son, Cadet George Archer-Shee.

My Lords deeply regret that they must therefore request you to withdraw your son from the College.

I am sir,
Your obedient Servant,
C. I. Thomas

The signatory, Charles Inigo Thomas, was Secretary to the Admiralty and his job was to see that decisions by the board were carried out. He was head of Administration and as a permanent feature in a world where most appointees, both political and naval, only served for a limited period, he had considerable influence.

The letter came as a stunning blow to Mr Archer-Shee. Until that moment he had never had any reason to doubt the character of his youngest son; he had always found him an honest and open boy, and this view was endorsed by his teachers at school before he went to Osborne. Since George was never to reach full maturity we cannot make a full assessment of his character, but the few who remember him recall that he was "an ordinary boy" with nothing particularly good or bad about him. He was the youngest in a big family and so by the firm parental standards of the day may have been a little spoilt from time to time, but not to any excess. He did not excel, but made the grade for most of the time. No one had ever found cause to suspect him of any dishonesty.

Mr Archer-Shee replied immediately:

N. – –11108

Bristol
18th October 1908.

Sir,

I have received the above 'confidential' letter calling upon me to withdraw my son Cadet George Archer-Shee from the Royal Naval College in disgrace as a thief!

Nothing will make me believe my boy guilty of this charge, which shall be sifted by independent experts.

Your obedient servant,
Martin Archer-Shee.

This letter went straight into the post, and the indignant writer prepared to travel to Osborne and to take steps to see that his promise of sifting by independent experts was carried out.

The Royal Naval College at Osborne on the Isle of Wight was still quite a new institution at the time, having only taken in its first batch of cadets six years before. It was the latest stage in over two centuries of development in training for command in the Royal Navy. Seafarers have long realised that to fit a man for responsibilities at sea it is necessary to 'catch him young'. From the time when Britain first had a standing navy in the days of Oliver Cromwell and the Protectorate, captains had made a practice of taking likely young men from their own families and from those of their friends to sea with them. They were nominally classified as 'servants' but were expected to learn the trade thoroughly and become officers themselves in due time. This practice was formally recognised after the restoration by the Lord High Admiral, the Duke of York, and made effective through Samuel Pepys, his remarkable protégé who was secretary to the Admiralty.

But gradually the Admiralty realised that training a man solely at sea was too limiting; while he would become a practical master of his trade he would lack a general education and a broad outlook on life. During the day to day running of a ship there was rarely sufficient time for the basic instruction necessary to give a grounding in such vital subjects as mathematics and navigation. In 1733 they opened a college for forty young gentlemen in Portsmouth Dockyard which gave pre-sea instruction in subjects ranging from the basic requirements to fencing and dancing. However this college was never the only means of entering the service. It was still possible for a young man to go straight to sea; one who started this way in the late eighteenth century was Horatio Nelson.

Nelson was the son of a humble Norfolk parson and he indicates the type of background from which many naval officer entrants came. The service was certainly not confined to the sons of the very rich, most of whom would have found the life too strenuous. Nepotism and influence was still important in getting selected but it had little influence on final promotion and postings. The sea is demanding and ignorance or incompetence will soon be shown up, perhaps with disastrous results. No captain had the money or space to carry passengers among his crew.

The Portsmouth Dockyard College provided a goodly proportion of the officers who led the fleet during the Napoleonic Wars, which at sea culminated in 1805 at Trafalgar. When peace had settled again there came one of those periods when Britain retrenches on her armed forces for economic reasons (false as history often proves this to be) and as a result the college was closed down in 1837. Once again everyone went straight to sea.

After a period of this, a number of captains expressed concern about the complete rawness of the recruits they were getting, both as officers and on the lower deck. In 1854, to help cure this, the Admiralty set aside a two-decker, HMS *Illustrious*, on which novice seamen would receive a year's preliminary training. Very shortly they realised that this would be equally valuable to trainee officers, who had been first called cadets around 1840. So successful did the whole idea prove to be that within a short time the seamen were squeezed out altogether. After eight years of service *Illustrious* was replaced by HMS *Britannia*, which from 1863 was permanently moored in the beautiful setting of Dartmouth Creek, making this Devonshire fishing village the centrepiece of naval education which it still is. However at the time captains at sea were asked for their views on the desirability of a shore college, and a substantial majority expressed themselves in favour.

It was to be nearly forty years before this was to be established. In the peaceful latter part of Queen Victoria's reign there seemed no urgency for it, but with the rise of the German navy at the turn of the century the matter had become more pressing. Dartmouth had proved an ideal site and King Edward VII laid the foundation stone of the college there in 1902. As a temporary measure, until the buildings were complete, the King gave the Navy permission to use part of the Crown estate at Osborne.

This had originated early in the reign of his mother, Queen Victoria. Wanting a country home where she could spend some time uninterrupted with her beloved husband Prince Albert and her family, she purchased a small house with magnificent grounds near East Cowes on the northern tip of the Isle of Wight. The existing house was far too small for the royal family and its entourage so it was torn down and a sizeable new mansion partly designed by Prince Albert himself took its place.

Whether or not the result is a thing of beauty is a matter of taste, but the fine sweeping grounds with a large number of varied trees which the Prince planted are a superb piece of English countryside. Victoria and Albert spent much time together here, and after Albert's death Victoria virtually retired to Osborne during her secluded widowhood. She died there in 1901.

Her fun-loving son Edward VII was not in the least interested in keeping on a place where he must have recalled some of the gloomier moments of his youth and so he wasted no time in getting rid of it by making a gift of it to the nation. Part of the building became a convalescent home for officers, while the state apartments were opened to the public and became an unequalled monument to overcluttered Victorian taste.

What the King offered to the Navy were some outhouses in the grounds about a quarter of a mile from the house together with a superb plateau for playing-fields. Additional temporary buildings were quickly put up and the first 'term' of cadets arrived at Osborne in 1903, for a two-year stay before going to Dartmouth for a further two years.

At the same time there were great changes both in the recruitment methods and in the actual education itself. On board the old *Britannia* instruction had concentrated largely on professional naval matters; new entrants were expected to have acquired the basic academic background when they arrived. As they normally entered at the early age of fourteen they usually had to go through a frenetic period of cramming beforehand to achieve the necessary standard, and naval educators felt that this was more intense than was good for young minds. Attempts to move the entry age up to sixteen were resisted by the public schools who would be supplying the bulk of the entrants: they said they did not want to lose a proportion of their cream half-way through their time with them.

The result was the decision that the Navy should have its own public school. Various ideas were correlated into what was known as the Selbourne Scheme, named after an able First Lord of the Admiralty in 1900 who had himself been a public schoolmaster. He was aided by two other remarkable and dedicated men, Professor J. A. Ewing, a brilliant engineer who had already advised the navy on some of the vital technical changes of the day including the introduction of the steam turbine engine, and Admiral Sir John Fisher. Reams have been written, and doubtless will continue to be written, about 'Jackie' Fisher, and though he plays only a minor direct part in this story no other man had more influence on the development of the navy at the beginning of the century. A man of outstanding intellect and dedication he tolerated neither fools nor those who differed with his views and inevitably made quite a number of enemies, though clearly at this time the Navy needed someone like him.

The Royal Navy had experienced no major fleet action between Trafalgar and the First World War, a gap of more than a century, and it would have been more than a miracle if the service had not grown a little torpid and out of practice over the years, particularly as it was also a period which saw the most traumatic changes in ships and weapons. Trafalgar was fought between wind-dependent wooden galleons whose muzzle-loading cannons threw a solid metal ball a distance measured in yards, while by the time of the First World War steam-powered steel-armoured ships had breech-loading guns which could lob a large explosive shell over the horizon.

The changes did not always come easily to tradition-minded men and there had been much in the way of new ideas and experience for them to accumulate. "What was good enough for Nelson is good enough for me" was still too often dominant in Naval thinking and it was often forgotten how progressive the great sailor had been in his own time, even advocating the adoption of steam in its very early days.

The scheme which was worked out for Osborne and Dartmouth was ingenious. Initially all cadets went to Osborne soon after their thirteenth birthday, the age at which they would otherwise have gone to public school, and then after two years they moved on to Dartmouth for a further two years. The Admiralty had hoped that the whole enterprise would be centred at Dartmouth, but it was some years before the building there was big enough.

Both colleges were organised the same way. In command of each was a captain, and immediately under him the staff organization split into halves, naval and civilian. A commander was in overall charge of the naval side and his chief subordinates were a number of 'term' lieutenants. All cadets who entered each term, usually around sixty in number, were grouped together rather in the way of a house at a public school, except they were all of a similar age. Their 'term' lieutenant, who would normally stay with them for their two years, was somewhat akin to a housemaster, looking after all out-of-class-room matters. He would organize games and recreation and maintain morale and discipline. He would be expected to have a strong loyalty towards his charges to make them into the leaders the Navy required, and to aid them as far as he could if they got into difficulties.

Each term officer had the assistance of a term petty officer, and these along with a number of naval pensioners as servants gave the young cadets their first contacts with the type of men they would have to command in the future. The naval staff also looked after such basic administrative requirements as pay and medical services, and they gave instruction in professional matters.

These always took second place to basic classroom work which was in the hands of a team of well-qualified schoolmasters under a head-master who, like the commander, reported directly to the captain. The headmaster was the able Charles Godfrey and his team included a number of dedicated professional teachers. However at this time the divided arrangement did not always work too well, mainly because the naval side tended to take too little notice of the aspirations of the civilian side to play its full part in college life, and the civilian side felt that some of the practices at the college were too naval for such young boys. One of them, Mr G. B. Smith, a young King's College man who taught English, recalls:*

> The Archer-Shee case was only one of many examples between 1903 and 1914 (when the Schoolmasters took over practically all of both sides of Osborne Administration) of the growing rift between the civilian masters and the junior officers. No other example got into the press, not even one of attempting to cure homosexuality by wholescale flogging, but they were frequent enough to put at risk the whole brilliant educational experiment which the Selbourne scheme involved.

However Mr Smith, who later became headmaster of Sedbergh and also taught at Repton and Eton, recalls that the period had its positive side:

> The generation of schoolmasters whom Charles Godfrey trained at Osborne between 1903 and 1914 became pioneers in the public schools in the years that followed. Huson and Upcott at Eton, Moorson and Bryant at Harrow, myself at Repton and Sedburgh, and many others. We had all learned from the naval officers how to manage boys, and five of us became public school headmasters.

This meant for the cadet that he had a sound basic education which prevented him from getting too narrow a view of life and also gave him something to come to fall back on if the navy failed him or he failed the navy. This was one of the main reasons why parents had to pay a fee akin to the current public school rate, though this was one aspect of the scheme which had not met with Fisher's approval, who felt that it would lead to recruitment from too narrow a segment of society.

This was the Osborne that Archer-Shee entered at the beginning of 1908. The Archer-Shee family had been formed in Ireland in the seventeenth century when Robert Shee and Rose Archer of Kilkenny married. Their first descendant to cross the water was a Martin

* Private letter to author.

A.A.A.—B

Archer-Shee, a budding artist who late in the eighteenth century came to London to study under Sir Joshua Reynolds; he later became a successful painter of the day and President of the Royal Academy.

His descendants included George's father who had started his own career in a more adventurous way than his later prosaic banking life would indicate. He had first joined the Chinese customs service and while there met and married a young New York girl Edith Pell. Their first son, to whom they also gave the name Martin, was born while they were in Canton. Mr Archer-Shee made an important friend when he got to know a rising young star of Britain's Colonial service, Evelyn Baring, the future Lord Cromer. Towards the end of the 1870s Baring was appointed British Commissioner of the Public Debt in Cairo, and started on his great work in Egypt, which he virtually ruled for over twenty years. Soon after he arrived there he invited Mr Archer-Shee to join with him as Inspector General of the Customs service.

This was rotten with graft which Mr Archer-Shee did what he could to reduce. Inevitably his moves were not always welcome, and after a while he fell so foul of established interests that he had to leave; this was in 1880. The exact details of the final row are lost, but Evelyn Baring wrote him a letter on his departure which starts:*

> 20 June 1880
>
> I write a line to express a hope that the circumstances under which you are leaving Egypt will in no wise stand in the way of your re-employment elsewhere, I consider that you have rendered a great service in introducing order and checking corruption in the Customs Department. That you and I have been subject to a good deal of criticism in doing it is inevitable—a reformer of your type can not hope to be popular.

Mr Archer-Shee does not seem to have had too much trouble in getting a new job; early in 1881 he joined the Bank of England as sub-agent in Birmingham. He spent seven years here learning the work of the Bank, during this time his wife died leaving him to look after a son and two daughters. In 1888 he was appointed Bank Agent in Bristol. Though he was sometimes referred to as Bank Manager, his work was much more akin to that of an area manager in a normal bank, and his particular job was to advise Threadneedle Street on economic developments in the West Country. Soon after he moved to Bristol he married again, this time an Englishwoman, Miss Treloar,

---

* In possession of Lieutenant-Colonel J. Archer-Shee: Reproduced by courtesy of the Earl of Cromer.

who gave him two more children, a daughter, and finally on 6th May 1895 another son, George. Both by nature and by calling Mr Archer-Shee was a man to whom honesty and integrity in financial matters were sacrosanct, and the suggestion that this young son of his was now both a thief and a forger would be particularly repugnant to him.

The Archer-Shee family was well-knit and comfortably off, devout Roman Catholics attending Mass regularly and making their confessions. George lived with them all the time in Bristol until he was eleven, when he was sent off to boarding school. He went first to Hodder which is the preparatory school for one of the leading English Catholic Public Schools, Stonyhurst, and then on to Stonyhurst itself. (On his first arrival he suffered some ribbing, for young schoolboy minds found the initials GAS painted on his trunk amusing.) Hodder and Stonyhurst nestle among the rolling Lancashire Dales in a fine old country mansion presented by a wealthy Catholic gentleman. Here he studied under a special Naval Class master, Mr Gordon Gorman, on whom he made a very favourable impression, and late in 1907 he sat the qualifying exam for Osborne.

The means of selecting cadets worked out under the Selbourne Scheme was to make all aspiring entrants sit a qualifying exam, and then all those who reached a satisfactory standard in this went for an 'interview'. At this they were confronted by a panel of senior naval officers who fired questions at them; the boy who could indulge in some forthright but courteous repartee stood a good chance; the procedure caused some amused public comment. Up to then an exam had been the only formal means of selection, though most entrants came on the recommendation of a senior serving officer; now an attempt was made to assess both their academic ability and their potential 'officer-like qualities'. Since later in his schooldays George was to be a lively figure in the debating society he presumably did not find this too difficult.

Though Osborne was the naval public school, in one important principle it differed from the normal public or any other school. While they existed for the benefit of the pupils, Osborne existed for the benefit of the Royal Navy. In view of the difficulty of assessing the potential development of character of a boy on the edge of puberty it was inevitable that the selection board would make some errors, or that some of their choices might be unable to keep up with the required academic work. Every parent had to give an undertaking that he would withdraw his son if requested to do so by the Admiralty; so important was this considered that the undertaking was included both on the entry form and on a separate sheet, both of which had to be signed. Conversely the parent had an obligation to ensure his son made a career in the Navy, and if he did not the Admiralty could make demands for compensation.

This was all to prove important in the complex legal arguments which took place later. It may in some ways seem to have been a one-sided arrangement, but to force a young man who is temperamentally unsuited for it into a life at sea will often lead to his eventual failure and personal unhappiness; families where there is a 'naval tradition' are sometimes guilty of this. 'Weeding out' took place at Osborne and around ten per cent of cadets were withdrawn, usually at the end of their first year. An occasional piece of gross misbehaviour would result in a summary request for withdrawal, akin to expulsion from a public school, but the criterion for deciding if any withdrawal was necessary would be that the cadet had proved himself unsuited to be a naval officer; a bit of ill-considered sky-larking would not qualify as this; 'official cuts' by a cane and the strong arm of a petty officer dealt with these occasions.

One other way in which Osborne differed from most public schools of the day was that science and technical subjects played a much more important part in the curriculum; the headmaster was usually a science teacher and more than half of his 'professional staff' specialized in science or mathematics. Though these subjects are vital to every ship's officer there was particular concentration at this time, as at the end of their training all cadets could be assigned to either the executive or engineering branch of the service. In theory they could also become Royal Marine Officers, though in practice few ever did this.

This arrangement was an attempt to solve a problem which had become apparent in the rapidly changing Navy. With the arrival of engines in ships had come engineers, but the traditional seamen or 'executive' officers had not found it easy at first to accept either the men or their machines. At first engines were only a supplement to sail and their overseers only came into their own when the captain had given the immortal order "Up funnel, down screw." For a long time snobbishness kept the engineers as second-class citizens and to try and overcome this the Selbourne Scheme created a common pattern of training.

It was soon no secret though that some parents were encouraging their offspring not to try too hard in their engineering studies, hoping that if they did not do too well in them they would be assigned to the executive branch. Among the cadets themselves it was considered creditable to become bottom in the engineering class. Though snobbishness was important in this, there was also the practical point that an engineer can never rise to the highest ranks and in particular can never achieve a command at sea, the main ambition of most who enter the Navy.* A few years later the engineers went back to recruiting and training separately.

The Admiralty were so sensitive about this that it was emphasised on the entry form which the parents had to complete that applicants could only be considered who were prepared to be assigned to any of the three branches. When Mr Archer-Shee completed the form for George he wrote in the appropriate place "Engineer or Executives preferred, Royal Marines if Necessary," but despite the very few cadets who ever went to the Royal Marines he had to amend even this to "Any of the three branches without reservation or qualification."

The Osborne at which George arrived early in 1908 seems on the whole to have been a happy and worthwhile place. The one-storey buildings created a pleasant bungalow atmosphere, even if they looked a bit temporary, and the grounds supplied the most magnificent surrounding scenery and playing-fields. In the temperate Isle of Wight climate there were plenty of opportunities for games and other outdoor activities which most boys enjoy so much.

Life for the boys could be tough; when on duty they had to move almost everywhere at the double, and they were not allowed a great deal of time to themselves. In education in general the residue of the sternest elements in Victorian thinking were still quite common, and any kid-glove methods in building young men for the Navy would have been quite unacceptable. Many of the customs of naval routine were introduced as well as the jargon; the floor was the 'deck', lavatories the 'heads' and leaving the college 'landing' or 'going ashore'. Discipline was imposed with some formality and even minor matters were 'offences' for which the offender was put on a charge; punishments at this time still included 'facing paint', standing for lengthy periods six inches from a wall without moving or speaking, though this was abolished soon afterwards.

Cadets were kept very much on their toes by the knowledge that

* This problem has continued to trouble the Navy for a long time and only very recently did an engineer reach the rank of full Admiral; he was Admiral Sir Francis Turner, coincidentally an old Stonyhurst boy.

what happened at Osborne could affect their whole career and their record would follow them throughout their service; any loss of time such as might happen if they failed their end-of-term exams and had to re-do some work could lead to long-standing loss of seniority. This despite the experience that outstanding cadets are by no means always those who go furthest in the service, and a number of those who have reached the highest rank were comparatively undistinguished at this stage. Life at Osborne had to be taken seriously; the college motto was *Disciplinâ, Fide, Labore*.

To greet George and the sixty or so other new cadets who arrived with him at the beginning of 1908 would have been the 'term officer', Lieutenant William Burrows. Burrows was a well-built man and a very able athlete who used to impress his charges with his feats in the gymnasium; he had specialised as a PT officer, a branch of the Navy which rarely attracts the brightest of officers: it is often a question of brawn over brain. Burrows does not emerge as a man with a forceful personality, and he probably went in some awe of his immediate superior the commander. Any new term officer was also a 'new boy' himself, and had to find his feet working mainly from previous experience in handling sailors, who were not always quite the same in their needs as cadets.

Each term was named after a noted historical figure, and George's was called 'Drake'. Over the years after they leave college the members will tend to keep at least distant contact with each other, and when possible meet up for term reunions; they watch each other's progress with interest and if an appreciable number of them reach high rank or distinguish themselves in some way then it is always a good boast to have been a member of that term. The member of 'Drake' with the most important future was probably T. H. Troubridge, a Second World War Admiral. Hugh Bousted, who got to know George quite well as their beds were near each other, also had a remarkable career, being the only man ever to be completely forgiven by the Royal Navy for what is usually regarded as the ultimate sin, desertion.*

Another early acquaintance for George would have been the master from the civilian side who was assigned to him as personal tutor to supervise his studies; each cadet had one, for George this was Mr C. H. C. Livesey, a senior science master and one of the more exper-

---

* Colonel Sir Hugh Bousted, KBE CMG DSO MC, tells his fascinating story in *The Wind of Morning*, Chatto & Windus, 1970, though his recollection of the details of this case are not always accurate.

ienced members of the civil staff. He was also greeted soon after his arrival by George Arbuthnot, another old Stonyhurst boy who had already been at Osborne a year and who was soon writing enthusiastic letters back to the old school, predicting that George might well come "top of his term".

Though George settled in quite satisfactorily this forecast was to prove over optimistic. In the summer at the end of his second term some of his teachers reported that his classroom performance was not up to standard and that they did not think he had the makings of a naval officer. The criticism was, however, solely of his classroom work and there is not the slightest evidence that the teachers or anyone else had any reservations about his character. The Admiralty sent a letter to Mr Archer-Shee warning that unless his son showed some improvement the Admiralty would be compelled to ask for his withdrawal, and suggesting that for the boy's sake provisional arrangements might be made for him to continue his education elsewhere.

This in no way put George in a unique position; quite a number of his fellow cadets' parents received similar letters and they did not always lead to the threatened withdrawal. Indeed, it was one of the hopes in sending them that they would give the boy a sufficient jolt, probably supplemented by a stern fatherly talk, to make him work harder; so when George returned for his third term in September he need not have been unduly worried by this. There is no record that anything else adverse had been said against him, and since later the Admiralty were scraping every barrel it is safe to assume that for the most part he had earned good opinions from those who had supervised him.

2
THEFT

It is pleasant on the Isle of Wight in autumn, and by Wednesday 7th
October 1908 the Christmas term at Osborne was well under way.
The main thing on George's mind that day was an engine. He had
seen a model steam engine in the catalogue of the well-known makers
of mechanical toys, Bassett-Lowke, which he very much wanted. His
father had been quite generous with his pocket money and so he could
easily afford it. He still had over £2 of the money he had brought
back to college at the start of term and the engine cost only 15s 6d.

But he did not have the cash in his hand; the college authorities did
not like cadets carrying too much money around with them, and so
that they could keep an eye on the way they spent it, it all had to be put
into a college bank at the start of term. Cadets' normal day-to-day
expenses were only for extra tuck, stationery and stamps which they
could buy from the college canteen, for which each boy was allowed to
draw 2s a week from the bank, but if he wanted more he had to get
special permission from his term officer. To buy such a sensible toy as a
model engine permission was easy to obtain and so immediately after
breakfast thatWednesday George scribbled on the flap of an envelope
"Can I have 16/– for an engine. Archer-Shee" and took it to Lieutenant
Burrows. He explained what he had in mind and the lieutenant quickly
added his signature.

He now had to go to the College Bank, kept by the Paymaster, who
did not open it until the afternoon. Immediately after lunch that day
all the cadets had to have a brief routine medical inspection; this was
over by two o'clock and then George took his chit along to the pay-

master and got his money. He then went to the college reading room where each cadet had a locker and put the money in there; his locker was the first in the second row, with an A at the beginning of his name he was first in alphabetical order. Next he went along to his dormitory to change into more informal clothes, for it was a half holiday, a "make-and-mend" in naval parlance, and he could spend the time as he chose.

Having changed he was a bit undecided. It was the timing of his movements from now on which later caused the bitterest arguments. He first wandered out of the building to a sheet of tarmac which surrounded the college flagpole; here every morning there would be the daily naval assembly, known as 'divisions', everyone would parade while the white ensign was slowly and smoothly hoisted to the top. Now a number of roller-skating enthusiasts had taken it over and were rattling round and round. George watched them for a short while and then decided to take the next step towards getting his engine, which was to buy a postal order from the Osborne Post Office. This was in the main Osborne House building a quarter of a mile from the college, and though so near, cadets did not go there often, for part of the route was 'out of bounds' and special permission was necessary. George had only been there once before.

Also watching the skating was a good friend of his, Patrick Scholes, and George suggested he should keep him company; Scholes briefly declined. George went back to the college on his own to collect his money from the reading room locker. By strict letter of the college law he was not supposed to go in there at that time as all the cadets were expected to be outside getting exercise and fresh air; but a quick visit would not be regarded as a serious breach of rules.

With the money he went outside and met Scholes again.

"Do come with me to the post office," he asked once more.

"No I can't," replied Scholes, and this time he added an explanation. "I've got some friends coming to see me. They are due at half past two."

It must have been almost this time at that moment, but George did not have a watch, still far too expensive an item in those days for a young man, and his knowledge of exact time was always a bit hazy. He decided to go alone and so he went to get the necessary permission; this had to be obtained from the duty petty officer who on that day was a senior veteran of the lower deck, Chief Petty Officer Paul, a man sincerely loyal to the service, but capable of becoming a bit excitable under stress, and not popular with the cadets. He readily gave George permission, admonishing him only to report when he got back. So George set out on his short, eventful, walk.

There was more than one way through the Osborne grounds to the post office and on the journey there George took the most direct route. As he was leaving the college a bell clanged in the distance, the sentry bell which sounded every half-hour, though not indicating in any way which hour.

At the end of the short walk he descended a flight of iron steps down to the post office which was in a deep basement. Inside the door a counter ran across the right side of the room and behind this a partition closed off another room. When George entered the only person there was a telegraph boy waiting for an errand. After a moment an elderly lady appeared behind the counter, Miss Clara Tucker who was in charge. Miss Tucker was to be a key figure in what followed and as far as can now be seen she was a typical member of the minor clerical class, conscientious and competent, but unimaginative and stubborn. No-one ever had any doubts about her honesty.

As she came out from behind the partition George asked for a fifteen-and-six postal order and a penny stamp. He gave her the sixteen shillings he had drawn from the bank and got threepence-halfpenny change. This puzzled him. Shouldn't it be fourpence? No, explained Miss Tucker, the postal order was for fifteen-and-six, plus a penny-halfpenny 'poundage' and a penny for the stamp. This taken from sixteen shillings left threepence-halfpenny change. She even went back to look in her till to check. Oh, explained George, he thought the 'poundage' on all postal orders was a penny: this is what it had been on the last one he had bought which had been for a much smaller sum. He then left.

At the top of the steps outside the post office the path split two ways. Both led back to the college and this time George decided to take the different route from the one he had come by; one of the results of this was that he turned straight into some shrubbery and so he could not see or be seen by anyone else coming up to the post office by the main route. He got back to the college, reported his return to CPO Paul, and went to the reading room to write his letter to Bassett-Lowke.

As he reached the door of the room he met one of his term-mates, Terence Back, coming out and looking a bit upset; they knew each other quite well for as their names were adjacent in alphabetical order their beds in the dormitory and their lockers were next to each other.

"I say, isn't it rot," exclaimed Back.

"I don't know what you are talking about," responded George.

"Why, I had a postal order taken out of my locker, and this is how I found my writing case." Back showed the case broken open.

That morning Back had been a cheerful boy for in the post he had received a five-shilling postal order, a present from a Miss Robinson, his aunt. He had shown this to a number of his envious fellows, and it was common knowledge that he had it. Now it was gone, for someone had broken into both his locker and the writing case inside which he had kept it. Unfortunately, such petty thieving was then not uncommon at Osborne and for some time had caused concern both to the authorities and parents; it had been reported well before George arrived.

George commiserated briefly with Back and then sat down at one of the tables to write his letter. When he came to fill in the postal order he was a bit uncertain what to do. Every postal order has three lines to be filled in. At the top there is a space for the payee and under this a line for the Post Office at which it can be cashed—filling this in is optional; at the bottom is a line with the word 'signature' under it which the payee signs when he cashes it. The system is about as insecure as it can be, for there is no attempt to match signatures, and anyone with a blank or incomplete postal order can fill in anything he likes.

But George was not quite certain what he had to do; he had sent off very few postal orders before. It was quite easy to see he must write "W. J. Bassett-Lowke Co" at the top, but what else? Should he sign somewhere, on the back perhaps? He turned and made an enquiry from his neighbour at the table, Cadet McNair, whose guidance cannot have been very clear, for George then wrote his name at the bottom on the line above the word 'signature' which should have been left blank for the recipient. He put it into an envelope with the letter and took it to the post; all he had to do now was to wait for his engine.

Nothing special happened for the rest of the day, and at 'pipe-down' time he turned in unconcerned. Next morning after getting dressed he took his usual look at the notice of daily orders, one of the pieces of standard naval routine instilled early into the cadets' experience. He found his name on this among a list of those who had to report to the commander immediately after breakfast; this was a regular session where the commander dealt with any minor matter which had come up.

Immediately after breakfast, which ended at half past eight, he went along to what was known as the 'Parents' Waiting Room' which was used as the interview room. He was possibly a bit apprehensive, and at least somewhat puzzled. A number of other cadets were also there waiting to see the commander, Commander Richard Stapleton-Cotton, who soon appeared. He was accompanied by his aid, the Cadet Gunner, David Gordon, an experienced warrant officer whose job was to help in smoothing along day-to-day administration in proper naval fashion.

Commander Stapleton-Cotton came from an aristocratic family, he was the second son of the second son of the second Viscount Combermere. Immediately before coming to Osborne, in 1907, he had served as a lieutenant in the royal yacht HMY *Victoria and Albert*. At the end of this tour of duty he was promoted to Commander (this was before the Navy introduced the intervening step of Lieutenant-Commander) and because he was known to the royal family was specially selected for the Osborne job when it was decided that the two royal boys, Prince Edward and Prince Albert, were to be sent there. Prince Edward, the future King Edward VIII and Duke of Windsor, arrived in 1907 two terms ahead of George, while Prince Albert, who became King George VI, joined the term after he left.

The Commander had sufficient personality to impress himself vividly on all at Osborne, and those who were there still clearly recall him, though not always very favourably. T. G. Bedwell, a member of the same term as Prince Albert, feels he was a bit of a bully, and not the right man to have charge of such young boys from good families because he was too bull-headed. This is confirmed by Mr R. B. Smith, then a young member of the staff, who says he was "bull-headed with horns" and that he came to Osborne with good intentions of being a new broom but only succeeded in setting everyone by the ears, and on a number of occasions caused severe commotions. However a fellow of George's in 'Drake' term, D. C. Morrison, regards him as having been "just the chap to bring up young officers." His philosophy was firmly the traditional one of the naval executive officer, "The Captain is God and I am his deputy;" everyone under him, cadets and junior staff, went in some fear of deputy-God.

In the waiting room that morning he left George until he had dealt with the minor matters concerning the other cadets. Finally he called the boy to him.

"Archer-Shee, did you go to the post office yesterday?"

"Yes sir."

"Did you cash a postal order?"

"No, I did not."

"But did you buy one?"

"Yes sir."

The Commander looked at him closely and pushed a piece of paper and a pen in front of him.

"Write down the name of your term-mate, Cadet Back," he instructed.

George wrote "Terence H. Back." The Commander studied this.

"Funny thing you should know Back's Christian name," he observed.

The Commander had been impressed by the way George wrote the name, using first Christian name and initial. Adolescent boys can be very formal in the address of each other, but the Commander did not seem to realise that George and Back had slept next door to each other and had had adjacent desks in class for a while, and so knew each other quite well. He had however another, rather personal, reason for thinking him a strong suspect.

What George is reputed to have replied was later one of the most bitterly argued points. The Commander claimed that he said he signed this way because he and Back and some others had been practising signing each others' signatures in the reading room a few days before; this is the sort of thing boys do for fun, but George afterwards never accepted that he had said this and Back denied that any such practice had taken place. (Whoever had signed the postal order had known that it was necessary to sign the name as written on the top line, and had just written "Terence Back".)

The Commander then concluded the interview for the moment.

"All right. Carry on," he instructed.

'Carry on' is the standard naval order to return to normal duties. For the moment that was what George did, not really knowing what the questions had all been about.

The next move took place about two hours later. George received another summons to see the Commander and this time things became a little clearer. He was now told that the signature he had written earlier had been compared with one on Back's stolen postal order and the writings were in the same hand. In addition, the Commander told him, the Postmistress claimed that the same cadet who had bought a fifteen-and-sixpenny order had also cashed the stolen five-shilling one. The matter, said the Commander gravely, was now in the hands of the captain. But, for the moment, once again, "Carry on".

George received his third call just after lunch, this time to the house of the captain of the college, Arthur Christian. Captain Christian was the man who had the overall responsibility for the 360 future naval officers at Osborne. He had distinguished himself early in his career in some gunboat diplomacy against obstinate African chieftains on the River Niger. He was quite new to his present post having only taken it up the previous July, and whether he was as good in this administrative job as in action seems open to question.

When George arrived at his house he found a number of people already gathered there, a very mixed bag. In addition to the Captain there was the Commander, Lieutenant Burrows his Term Officer, the Assistant Paymaster, Mr Spickernell, and Postmistress, Miss Tucker; also some half-dozen other cadets including his fellow old Stonyhurst boy George Arbuthnot.

The Captain started with what must have seemed a rather pointless process. While everyone else looked on he interrogated each cadet in turn, asking them unimportant questions about nothing in particular. He asked George what he had done the previous Sunday. The boy was a bit hazy about this; first he thought he had gone for a walk, but then he remembered he had been a bit unwell and spent the day in bed. Whatever, the details seemed immaterial to the Captain.

Then all except Back, Arbuthnot and George were told to sit down. These three were asked some more questions, with the Captain turning finally to George; he showed him Back's name which he had written down for the Commander that morning.

"Did you write this?"

"Yes sir."

"But," and the Captain brought out a five-shilling postal order and pointed to the name Terence Back written along the bottom, "did you write this?"

"No sir."

Finally he was asked a few, not very many, questions about his movements the previous afternoon. He explained he had gone to the post office and he thought this must have been about half past two, certainly it was half past something, because he had heard the sentry bell; he agreed that it might have been half past three. He did not feel he had been quizzed at all thoroughly when the interrogation came to an end. Apart from the Captain no-one else took any part in it, and George's supposed guardian angel, Liutenant Burrows, made no effort to intervene or advise him. One thing he was not asked was if he had any money on him now. When the Captain was finished he was just told to wait outside.

Then after half an hour, and with nothing more said to make it clear what this was all about, once again he was told:

"Carry on."

He carried on this time for some days without hearing anything more about the matter. For the most part George was not the worrying kind and only one college-mate could later recall that he said anything about the event, when changing for games a few days later he made a casual reference to the fact that he thought he was a suspect. Most of the other cadets had no idea anything was wrong.

What caused him just as much conern was something he discovered the next day, Friday. At about a quarter to seven that evening he went along to this dormitory to change after engineering class and found that the hasp which secured the money till in his sea chest had been broken; it had been all right when he had been there three hours before. He reported the matter to Cadet Gunner Gordon, but nothing was discovered.

A further week and more passed before he heard anything new at all; there was no more interrogation and he was given no hint how enquiries were progressing. When he did get some news it came in a rather unusual way. Ten full days after the last enquiry, in the morning of Monday 19th October, he received a pair of telegrams from his family saying they were on their way to collect him and take him away.

He was put more clearly in the picture soon afterwards by a call to see Captain Christian, for the first time since the original enquiry. The Captain told him shortly that the Admiralty was satisfied he was responsible for the theft of the postal order and had decided he must leave the college at once. Until his parents arrived to collect him he was to take no further part in any college activity and was to remain 'isolated' from the other boys.

The Captain then shed a few crocodile tears.

"I am very sorry about it and I am not sure that you wrote that order, but I have no doubt that you cashed it."

This was a curious observation since an important part of the case against George had been the Commander's estimate that the signature was in his handwriting. If now the Captain did not accept this, but still believed George was involved then he had made no attempt to discover George's accomplice who had been the forger. Once more he repeated to George that the Admiralty had ordered his dismissal.

"All I can say is that I did not do it," firmly protested the boy once again. He then left for 'isolation' until his father appeared.

He was placed in the parents' waiting-room, and to make quite sure he remained isolated a Royal Marine sentry with rifle and bayonet was stationed outside the door. Despite this, when another cadet of his term, Morrison, heard of his plight he got some sweets from the tuckshop and managed to smuggle them in.

Mr Archer-Shee arrived at the college around dusk, a little earlier than he was expected for instead of taking the steamer which most arrivals from the mainland travelled on he was too impatient, and hired a special tug. He brought with him his elder son, George's half-brother Major Martin, who was 22 years the boy's senior. When the pair arrived at the college and made themselves known George was quickly produced.

"I want to see the Captain," demanded Mr Archer-Shee.

This proved more difficult. It seemed that the authorities had hoped that he would depart with his son and no fuss. The three were put into the parents' waiting room until the Commanding Officer could make himself available. They were left there alone for quite a period and inevitably Mr Archer-Shee and Major Martin used the time to find out from George just what had happened. In the circumstances the boy's story was not very clear, but on one point he was adamant: he had had nothing at all to do with the theft or forging of any postal order. His manner was such that both father and brother were convinced he was telling the truth.

Eventually the Captain condescended to see them, though they soon realised this was to be a mutual waste of time. The Captain made it clear that he was going to shelter behind 'higher authority': the matter had been decided by the Admiralty and he could not discuss it. Any queries must be addressed to them. The impression he succeeded in giving was that he had played little part in reaching the decision. But, Mr Archer-Shee demanded, what was the evidence against his son? Sorry, he was told, you must ask the Admiralty. The indignant father then got very angry and the meeting ended in a tautly strained atmosphere; the Captain's evasiveness made him even more convinced of the need for a thorough investigation.

There was nothing more that could be done there and so all three left the college, George clearly showing how unhappy he was. Those who closed the gates behind them presumably thought that that was an end to the matter. If so they completely failed to take into account the stubborn determination of the Archer-Shees and some powerful help they could enlist; it was to be almost three years before everything was finally settled.

3

MEANWHILE BACK
AT THE COLLEGE...

The main difficulty Mr Archer-Shee faced at first was that he had only an incomplete idea of the evidence which led the authorities at Osborne and at the Admiralty to conclude that George was the thief. His son could only explain what he had gleaned at the various investigations. It was clear that the postmistress, Miss Tucker, had given important information, and also that some comparison had been made of handwritings, but apart from this the picture was cloudy. Captain Christian had emphasised that the final decision had been taken in London.

What Mr Archer-Shee did not know was that the first mention of his son's name as a suspect had occurred very early on, at the moment when Terence Back had first reported the theft to CPO Paul. As soon as he discovered the postal order missing Back had told virtually everyone he met, and Paul first heard about it from another cadet, Butt. He immediately sent for Back to get the details, and somewhere in this conversation the name Archer-Shee was mentioned. Who introduced it first is not clear, but Paul would have known which cadets had been to the post office that afternoon as he had given the necessary permission; Back later denied making any suggestion at this point that he thought George could be the thief. Whoever did bring the name in, however, sowed the first seed of suspicion for no obvious good reason.

CPO Paul straight away reported to the Cadet Gunner who sought out the Commander; when he told him a most interesting conversation took place:

"A postal order has been stolen, sir."

"Anyone suspected?"

"Yes sir, Cadet Archer-Shee."

"A Catholic, of course,"★

This prejudiced reaction was widely known among staff at Osborne at the time, though it never escaped into the hands of the Archer-Shees or their advisers. Had they known it there is no doubt they could have made much of it, and the general criticism of the handling of the matter at Osborne would have been even stronger.

The Commander acted quickly, hoping perhaps that this time he could lay by the heels a troublesome thief who had been at large in the college for some time. Early in the evening he telephoned the post office where he was answered by Miss Barlow, Miss Tucker's assistant, who soon realised that what he was asking about was a matter which had occurred when Miss Tucker was on duty, and so she passed the call over.

The Commander told Miss Tucker that a five-shilling postal order payable to a Terence Back had been 'lost' and asked if she could help. Miss Tucker replied that she would look into the matter and call back. She went to the drawer where all postal orders cashed that day had been put and soon found the order in question, seemingly cashed by Terence Back. She rang the Commander back and said it was "all right", the order was safe and had been cashed. Apart from telling him this, she indicated she was not willing to talk about the matter over the telephone.

The Commander then despatched CPO Paul to see her. A few minutes later a rather flushed and agitated Paul arrived in the post office; Miss Tucker described him later as being in "a very flustered" state and almost "raving". He clearly made an unfavourable impression on her as he forcefully expressed views about "such people not being wanted in the Navy" and therefore he was not very effective in securing the lady's co-operation. As she put it "he had a lot to say, I took no notice of him". Subsequently there was to be some doubt if Paul had specified that a cadet was under suspicion, but Miss Barlow recalled that he talked about a "boy" signing the order. Not getting very far, Paul felt that a ring or two of gold braid might secure more respect and co-operation, and so he said that an officer would probably come next.

This was Cadet Gunner Gordon, who went there early the following morning. He did not get very much further than Paul, except that

★ Private letter from Mr G. B. Smith to the author.

Miss Tucker gave him the number of the postal order in question. He asked her if she would come up to the college to see the Commander and she agreed to do this during the morning.

Meanwhile at the college the Commander had been making other enquiries and the most important information he had unearthed was that only two cadets had obtained permission to go to the post office during the afternoon. The other one besides George was Arbuthnot, who said he had gone there both to cash and buy postal orders shortly after two o'clock.

Miss Tucker made her promised visit to the college soon after ten o'clock, bringing the postal order with her. She was questioned by the Commander and she now volunteered the information that she recalled only two cadets coming in the previous afternoon. The first one soon after two o'clock had cashed one postal order and bought two, the second, an hour or so later, she claimed, had cashed the Terence Back five-shilling order and bought one for fifteen-and-sixpence. She recalled, in particular, that the visit of the first cadet had been punctuated by a Mr De Smit, one of the officers staying at the convalescent home who had some telegrammes to send off; she had kept the cadet waiting while she dealt with these. The Commander then enquired if she thought she would be able to identify the cadets, and she replied that they all looked alike to her, but she did think she might recognise a voice. When she had told the Commander all she could she returned to the post office.

Commander Stapleton-Cotton now saw George for the second time and then reported to Captain Christian both verbally and in writing. The Captain decided to act immediately and Cadet-Gunner Gordon went back to the post office soon after mid-day to ask Miss Tucker to come up to the college again. She was out when he got there so he left a message with Miss Barlow, asking her to come and see the Captain at soon as she could. Miss Tucker received this about half past one, and immediately went back to the college.

After a short wait there she was taken to the Captain's house where he explained he wanted her to try and identify from among a group of cadets either of the two who had been in the post office the day before. Some six or seven boys in uniform were brought into the room, and Miss Tucker looked at them carefully. Then the Captain got each one to talk by putting some general questions; at this point he did not himself know which was the boy under suspicion; his position was too remote for him to know individual cadets by name.

When he had talked to each boy they were sent out of the room and Miss Tucker confessed that she could not identify any of them either by appearance or voice. She still insisted though that the stolen postal order had been cashed by the same boy who had bought one for fifteen-and-sixpence.

The Captain asked the Commander which of the boys was Archer-Shee and he was brought back in and questioned further. But this did not help Miss Tucker at all. The lady was then allowed to return to the post office and during the afternoon a formal statement giving a brief summary of what she had said was prepared and taken down to the post office for her to sign. The first copy shown to her she objected to because she was described as 'Postmistress'. "No," she insisted with the typical stubbornness of minor officialdom, "I am Clerk-in-Charge." The document was then taken back to the college for retyping and she signed it when it brought back to her, then filed a report about the incident with her superiors and forgot the matter. Her statement read:

I, Miss A. C. Tucker, the Clark-in-Charge at Osborne Branch Office, am positive that only two Cadets came to do business with Postal Orders on the afternoon of Wednesday, 7th October, 1908.
The first one cashed a Postal Order for 10/- and bought one for 12/3 and another for 2/6.
The second bought a Postal Order for 15/6 and cashed one for 5/-.
I swear that the Cadet who bought the Postal Order for 15/6 also cashed one for 5/- which was made payable to, and was signed 'Terence Back'.

> A. C. Tucker,
> Clerk in Charge
> Osborne Branch Office

At the college Captain Christian and Commander Stapleton-Cotton concluded that the case against George was proved. They made no effort to find the missing money by searching him or his locker or chest, nor did they enquire to see if he had made any unusually high purchases at the college Tuck Shop. They just allowed him to resume normal college life while they prepared their report. This took the form of a letter to the Commander-in-Chief at Portsmouth:

> Royal Naval College,
> Osborne
> 8th October, 1908

Sir,
    I regret to have to report a serious case of stealing a Postal Order by a Cadet on the 7th Instant.
    On the afternoon of the 7th Instant Cadet Terence H. Back (3rd Term) reported to the Cadet Gunner that he had lost a Postal Order for 5/- out

of his locker in the Reading Room. The Order had been sent to him by his people, and was made payable to him (Terence Back).

Cadet Back states that four or five Cadets saw him place the Order in his locker, and of these Cadet Archer-Shee was one.

The Cadet Gunner reports that only two Cadets obtained permission to go to Osborne House Post Office during the afternoon for the purpose of dealing in Postal Orders: they were Cadet James G. Arbuthnot (6th Term) and Cadet George Archer-Shee (3rd Term).

Miss Tucker, the Clerk-in-Charge at Osborne Post Office, stated to me that she quite well remembered the two Cadets coming in yesterday. One had cashed a Postal Order for 10/- and bought two others between 2 and 2.30 p.m., and the other about 3.30 p.m. had bought a Postal Order for 15/6 and had also cashed one for 5/- which was payable to Terence Back, and bore the signature of Terence Back. Of this she is quite positive, and her statement is attached. The Postal Order has been brought up for my inspection, and the signature thereon is as stated.

Miss Tucker is also certain that no other Cadets came to the Post Office during the afternoon.

Cadet Arbuthnot stated that having obtained permission from the Cadet Gunner he went over to Osborne House Post Office immediately after the Medical inspection (2 p.m.) and cashed a Postal Order for 10/- and also bought one for 2/6 and another for 12/3 for another Cadet.

Cadet Archer-Shee states that after the Medical Inspection he watched the other Cadets roller-skating, but between 3 and 4 p.m., having asked permission he went to the Osborne House Post Office and bought a Postal Order for 15/6. He positively denies that he cashed a Postal Order for 5/- and also denies that the signature on the Postal Order was written by him.

At 2 p.m. today the Clerk-in-Charge, Miss Tucker, came over and I had six Cadets fallen in of whom Archer-Shee was one, but she was unable to identify him as the Cadet who had cashed the Postal Order for 5/- payable to Cadet Back.

In my opinion Cadet Archer-Shee undoubtedly took the Postal Order from Back's Locker and cashed it at the Post Office, and I beg to submit that he should be withdrawn forthwith the College.

> I have the honour to be,
> Sir,
> Your Obedient Servant,
> A. H. Christian,
> CAPTAIN

Miss Tucker's statement was attached to this and the same day the two documents were sent off. The following morning they reached the Commander-in-Chief, Admiral Sir Arthur Fanshaw at Admiralty House in Portsmouth Dockyard, but he concluded this was not a matter for him, and so he sent them straight on to the Admiralty in London.

Here they were placed on the most important desk of all, that of the First Lord, Mr Reginald McKenna. The Government of the British Navy has often been the subject of wry comment, notably by W. S. Gilbert in *H.M.S. Pinafore*, because the First Lord of the Admiralty, "the ruler of the Queen's Navee," is always a civilian who probably knows very little about the sea. He is a professional politician, a leading Minister of the Crown appointed by the Prime Minister. If Gilbert may have made fun of the seeming absurdities of this system, it had its advantages. British politicians are accustomed to working closely with professional advisors in fields where their knowledge is thin and knowing when advice has to be taken, and it also means that the professional heads of the Navy, the Sea Lords, do not have to get too close to current politics, and can work loyally and impartially with an administration of any political colour. Even so imperious a sailor as 'Jackie' Fisher, who was by now First Sea Lord, never had any real difficulty in working within this system, he always respected the rights of the politician, his First Lord, to be advised on any important matter.

Indeed, Fisher at the time had a particularly close and friendly working relationship with Mr McKenna, still quite a new First Lord. Mr McKenna came from Ireland, where his father had been a convert from the Catholic faith to Protestantism. He trained as a lawyer and entered Parliament when he was thirty-two in 1895 as a Liberal at a time when his party was starting a long period out of power. During this time McKenna diligently polished up knobs on big front doors, and his potential was soon spotted by Sir Charles Dilke, a leading Liberal whose own position in the front of the political scene had been permanently scarred by a divorce scandal, but who retained some party influence. When in 1905 the Liberals swept to power with a massive majority McKenna was made Financial Secretary to the Treasury. Two years later he got his own department as President of the Board of Education, and in a Cabinet reshuffle in April 1908 he became First Lord.

The Government he served in is as remarkable as any which have governed Britain in the twentieth century. For good or ill, it was headed at first by Sir Henry Campbell-Bannerman, who died after two years, and then by Mr Herbert Asquith who took his place. The Liberals after so many years out of office were itching for a chance to put into operation some of the ideas they had developed, in particular they wanted to initiate Britain's first steps in what is now known as social security, where the flamboyant Welsh "wizard" Lloyd-George led the way, aided and abetted by the young turncoat Tory Winston Churchill. Many of their proposals were to provoke the bitterest opposition and this was to lead to one of the hottest political seasons ever in British history.

The Navy was often in the thick of this. Fisher's reforms, in particular the building of a considerable number of the powerful new modern battleships, 'Dreadnoughts', had provoked fierce controversy both inside and outside the service. Many Britons of varying political views, were becoming alarmed at the growing military and naval might of Germany, and the bellicosity of Kaiser Wilhelm, and they wanted to be prepared for a major clash. The newly-founded Navy League was running its ultimately successful "we want eight and we won't wait" campaign for the building of more Dreadnoughts. In the Cabinet these demands were not easily accepted by the radical reformers who wanted as much of the available money as possible to spend on their social experiments.

McKenna however concluded, to the intense irritation of Lloyd-George and Churchill, that the German threat was to be taken seriously, and fully supported his Sea Lords in all reasonable demands. His weakest personal point was that he lacked deep political warmth, he had a mind which is described as seeing everything in figures, he was the best chess player in the House of Commons. He had great confidence in his own personal judgment, far too great according to his critics, and he was probably a more successful First Lord in the corridors of the Admiralty than on the front bench in the House of Commons. A young Conservative member, Mr F. E. Smith, noted that he was one of the most unpopular members of the Government on their side. This is one main reason why his promising political career did not last very long, and he ended his working life in other fields.

When Captain Christian's letter about George reached him his trained legal mind noted that evidence was not quite as conclusive as the Osborne authorities seemed to think. A note was made on the margin of Miss Tucker's statement (probably by McKenna himself) "But she could not identify him." McKenna later claimed that he had immediately realised the serious consequences of the accusation for the boy and felt the least he could do was to give him a chance. He decided to call for a handwriting report, to see if this would confirm that the signature on the stolen postal order had been written by George.

A telegram went to Osborne asking that the postal order and some samples of both George's and Back's handwriting should be sent to London. The postal order had to be obtained from the post office which lent it on condition it was returned.

The leading handwriting expert of the day was Mr Thomas Gurrin. The 'Expert' was at the time a recent arrival in British courts; science had advanced in the latter part of the nineteenth century to a position where it could often aid the criminologist, and public imagination had been captured by the use of science by Sir Arthur Conan Doyle's great fictional creation, Sherlock Holmes. The trouble at this time, it is now realised, was that some of these experts were allowed by the courts to trade too much on their reputation; they could go into the witness box and make assertions which counsel rarely had the knowledge to challenge or probe properly.

In the case of handwriting there is always an element of intuition in reaching conclusions, and Mr Gurrin had got himself into a position where the courts and others listened with great respect to his views, despite the fact that he had been proven badly wrong on at least one notable occasion. A few years before these events he had given strong supporting evidence which helped in the conviction of Adolf Beck for defrauding women; this is one of the most notorious miscarriages of justice in British legal history, and it was only after Beck had served one five-year term in prison and had been convicted a second time that it was shown beyond doubt that it was a case of mistaken identity. Yet Mr Gurrin had asserted that Beck had written some letters which were eventually shown not to be his.

He still had his reputation, and was regularly consulted by the Home Office and other government departments. He was now contacted and agreed to give an opinion as soon as he could, on his return to London from giving evidence in a case at Gloucester Sessions. This was towards the end of the week, when he set about examining the postal order and comparing it with the specimens of George's and Back's handwriting.

It is clear that in his briefing Mr Gurrin had had an indication that George was a suspect. No attempt was made to get an impartial identification by submitting a number of anonymous handwriting samples, which would have been a more scientific and fairer way of doing things. His report to Mr McKenna read:

> At the request of the secretary to the Admiralty I have this day—the 17th October 1908—examined a Postal Order for 5/- number F/49 450659 made payable to Terence Back, Osborne Post Office, and I have compared

the signature namely Terence Back written under the words "Received the above-named sum" with the three written specimens of a hand-writing attached thereto which I understand are the handwriting of G. Archer-Shee, and from my comparison I cannot resist the conclusion, which I base on the similarity of the handwriting, both as regards the form of the letters as well as the angle of inclination, the pen pressure and the general character, that the signature Terence Back referred to on the second postal order was written by the same person who wrote the three speci-mens to me for confirmation.

To justify the expression of this opinion I add that I have been con-tinuously engaged in the examination of disputed handwriting since the year 1884 and that I have been frequently called upon by the Home Office and Treasury Authorities to give evidence on questions of handwriting.

Thomas Henry Gurrin,
Fellow of the Royal Microscopical Society,
Bath House, Holborn Viaduct,
London, E.C.
October 17th 1908.

Today in court a lawyer would ask Mr Gurrin to elaborate, to give some comparative examples of the form of the letters and the angles of inclination. Comparing the two postal orders, the one with some writing which is by George and the other with the forged signature shows that there is indeed a surface similarity between the two writings, they look as if the authors had learnt from the same copybook, but a close examination reveals a substantial difference in detail. Compare the 'B' of Bassett in the postal order written by George with the 'B' of Back on the other one, and the way these letters connect up with the following 'a' (see illustrations between pages 56 and 57).

It had however been suggested to Mr Gurrin that the writing on the stolen postal order was disguised or that whoever had cashed it took the unnecessary step of trying to copy the writing on the payee line. In a modern study of handwriting identification* Dr Wilson Harrison of the Home Office Forensic Laboratory at Cardiff observes "Where disguise is confidentially expected he [the document examiner] will run the very real risk of making an incorrect identification of the writer by lightly dismissing as disguise any consistent dissimilarities which otherwise he would attribute to different authorship. This facile tendency to shrug off any differences as due to disguise lies at the root of the notorious errors of judgment made by some of the 'handwriting experts' of a former generation." Dr Harrison then goes on to cite the Beck Case as a particularly well-known example.

* *Suspect Documents* by Wilson R. Harrison, Sweet & Maxwell, 1958.

Nevertheless when, on Saturday 17th October, this report by Mr Gurrin reached the Admiralty they were completely satisfied that it supported Captain Christian's views, and so they immediately wrote to Mr Archer-Shee, and also told Captain Christian that his recommendation was accepted.

At Osborne few of those not directly concerned had had any idea what was going on. The civilian staff heard the news with both surprise and annoyance. Though such disciplinary matters were not their direct concern they were irritated at not being consulted at all and also at the seemingly high-handed way the naval side had acted on what looked like slender evidence.

When Mr Livesey, George's personal tutor, learned of it he told his class, which was the first news they received. As he did so he added a comment, which the boys noted, reflecting his own view of the matter.

George's term mates were shocked by the news. They just could not believe that George was a thief; they knew him well and in such close circumstances boys have a good opportunity to form an opinion of each other. Later in the day a group of them were discussing it in the reading room when they decided to do something. They would send George a joint letter of sympathy. This they did, and 45 signed, many with their nicknames. Today it reads as a fascinating example of Edwardian schoolboy terminology:

> R. N. College,
> Osborne
> 19.10.08

Dear Shee,

You don't know how sorry we are about your bad luck. Your tutor Mr. Livesey told us in class that he did not think you did it. You were awfully plucky about it. We hope your pluck will be rewarded. It is a deuced mob here without your jibes.

We enclose one of your book plates which you left behind. The things that you left with G. Startin will be sent off on Saturday. He also got a roll of undeveloped films for you.

We do not know how to send off this letter so good-bye with a hairy jibe.

> We remain,
> H. R. Bland (rurtoie, Monkey) (Hairy).
> J. P. Money.
> J. B. Cole-Hamilton.
> F. H. Powys-how-am-you!!!
> Q N R(2) (B.J.C.).
> R. B. Squoggage.
> G. T. Philip.

J. H. MacNair (Pelican).
G. Startin.
Squit. $\dfrac{\text{R.N.}}{\text{Toast.}}$ (L.G.C.T.)
J. W. Harves.
R. L. B. Camel (deuced mob)
F. C. Miller.
K. M. Greig (beer barrel).
F. A. Hall (Fish-Wife)
H. P. Scholes (Jimmy Whats your name).
J. G. Y. Loveland   intermediate cylinder
Bullock (E. F. L.)
Cadets, Shun! (B. Dean)
A. M. Carrie (Giddy Belch)
Nines.
Beaky (C. A. Kershaw)
Nellie Weekes (Stick it in).
Cockroach (Cochrane).
A.B.C. (Carnegie).
Stinksly (T.H.W.)
Griffiths (Griffin)
Cupid (W.H.)
Metcalfe (W.B.)
L. V. Donne.
Leo (F.C.L.)
Turkish Delight. (L.C.J.E.)
Scab. (M.W.T.)
Cable (G.M.K.W.)
The Butler (C.M.B.)
H-H-H-H-a-a-m and eggs (P.M.B.H-H-H-)
Gurlie (G.J.L.)
Limestone (D.W.G.)
Mad One (A.C.G.M.)
Sleep Walker (E.M.T.)
Dirty Wench (H.F.E.)
J. H. Hansard.
Slack Dog (G.T.A.S.)

4
INTO ACTION

Many years after these events a young lady was about to marry into the Archer-Shee family as the bride of one of Major Martin Archer-Shee's sons. She was taken to meet her future mother-in-law who by this time was old and ailing, but despite this the young lady approached with the diffidence any girl has when meeting her future mother-in-law for the first time. It took the old lady a while to comprehend whom she was meeting, but when at last she did she looked up and observed:

"You know, my dear, you are marrying into a very difficult family."

Perhaps a more apt word for difficult would have been stubborn, for with their Irish heritage it is an Archer-Shee characteristic that once set on a course they persue it over all obstacles to the bitter end; also significant is the family motto, *Vincit Veritas*, which means 'Truth Conquers'.

By this time George's father was past sixty, not in the best of health and thinking of retiring from the bank before too long. In these circumstances it is doubtful whether, despite his determination to obtain justice for his son, he would have had the energy to see the matter through all that was to follow. However in his elder son Major Martin he had an ally with all the youth and vigour needed, and at least equal determination. Despite their great difference in ages, 22 years, the two half-brothers had been quite close, and had written to each other periodically when George was away at school or at Osborne.

The Major was then 36 years old. Like his young brother he had started out with ambitions to make a naval career, but this too had been thwarted though for a very different reason. He had successfully completed training in the old HMS *Britannia* moored in Dartmouth estuary, but when he had gone to sea he discovered he suffered from acute and incurable seasickness. This is no joke, as any sailor knows, and can be a serious handicap to the efficient performance of duties, so he left the Navy and turned to the Army.

He served in the South African war with some distinction, winning the DSO at the siege of Ladysmith. After this he spent a spell as the adjutant of the Cavalry school, but when in 1905 he was refused leave to go to New York to get married he decided he had had enough of soldiering and left the service. His marriage strengthened the family's American connections for his bride, like his mother, came from there: she was indeed also a Pell, a distant cousin of his mother's. The Pells are descended from John Pell, an ambassador of King James I to the Vatican whose loyal service was rewarded with a plot of land in the 'Colonies' where he started the American family. At some later date one of them married an American Indian, a princess of the Wompage tribe, from which they acquired certain physical family characteristics: they all tend to be tall and have a small gap between their front teeth.

Out of the Army Major Martin turned to politics. Inevitably he had a strong interest in one major political issue of the time, Ireland, and any Irishman's political affiliation depended on one question, whether he was a Unionist, in favour of the continued Government of Ireland from Westminster, or a Nationalist who wanted power transferred to Dublin. The division was usually on religious lines, with most Catholics Nationalist and Protestants Unionist; however Major Martin was an unusual exception as he was a Catholic Unionist. The family were always loyal to their faith, and Major Martin's two sisters, Mary and Winifrede, had both entered the Sacred Heart Order as nuns.

To peruse his political ambitions Major Martin became an active member of the Conservative and Unionist party, then forming an unusually small opposition in the House of Commons, and he also studied some law. From 1907 he nursed the London Parliamentary seat of Finsbury with a view to wresting it from the incumbent, a Labour member, at the next election. In these activities he inevitably got to know a number of influential people to whom he could now turn for help.

Major Martin was a spare upright man, in both appearance and character; his soldier training was clear from his military bearing. Once started on any course of action he would stick to it with tenacious determination until he had achieved his original aim. The battle to clear his brother was not to be the only occasion in his life when he took on authority and pursued it to eventual victory; later he had a protracted battle with the Inland Revenue. If ever in the months that were to follow anyone else had doubts about whether the continued fight was worth the effort and expense, it would be Major Martin who would insist on no retreat.

It was immediately after they had all left Osborne that Major Martin had the inspiration which was to prove crucial to the final outcome.

"There is only one person who can help you," he told George, "Carson."

Today at the end of a wide pathway leading from the Northern Ireland Parliament Building, Stormont, near Belfast, stands a statue of a tall cadaverous-featured man with one hand pointing upward, the other splayed slightly to the side. This is the tribute from the people of Northern Ireland to the man to whom today for good and ill they owe their separate existence from the rest of Ireland, still tied to the United Kingdom.

Surprisingly Edward Carson was not a Belfast or even an Ulsterman at all. He was the second son of a moderately successful architect in Dublin where he had been born in 1854. As a boy he first showed interest in following his father's profession, but his father was not happy about this, feeling either that creating buildings did not bring adequate rewards or that Edward was not cut out for it, so he directed his son's interests towards the law. He sent him to that great university, Trinity College Dublin.

There young 'Ned' Carson did well, without making any outstanding mark; his greatest successes were on the floor of the Historical Society, as the University Debating Society was named. One of his contemporaries at Trinity, though never a close friend, was a flamboyant young aspirant dramatist whose path was to cross his traumatically some years later, Oscar Wilde.

After he was called to the Irish Bar Carson found his first few years when he was learning the practical side of the business as lean as they are for most young barristers. Eventually work started to come in and he began to make a name as a persuasive advocate. When he was in his early thirties he was well established, and was given the official position of Crown Prosecutor for Ireland. Soon afterwards he was offered a seat on the Irish bench and there seemed every likelihood that this was the way he would end his career. But he hesitated, thinking there might be greater opportunities if he stayed free, though there is nothing to suggest he had any of those visions of great destiny which some men claim.

The opportunity did come, quite soon. At that time Trinity College was allowed to send two members to the House of Commons at Westminster, and in 1891 one of these seats fell vacant. Carson was prevailed on to stand for it. In most political matters Carson could be called a moderate radical, but he was a Protestant and so on the one vital question of the time, the relationship of Ireland with Great Britain, he was an almost fanatical unionist.

He faced his electorate as a Liberal Unionist, which meant he was allied to the Conservative party, and won against a more rigid Conservative opponent. The Conservative party was in power when he got to Westminster, and in urgent need of an Irish lawyer to fill the post of Solicitor General for Ireland, so Carson was given the job straight away, and had the unusual experience of taking his seat for the first time on the Government front bench. This did not last long, and he had not even made his maiden speech when the Government fell and he had to move over to opposition. Here he soon earned a reputation as one of the foremost advocates in Parliament of the Unionist cause.

Members of Parliament were unpaid in those days, and so to keep himself and his family he took another unusual step for an Irish barrister, he began to practise at the English Bar. Not all Irish advocates can do this successfully for the English courts tend to react against two common Irish faults, a tendency to bully and an excess of blarney. Carson, who rarely got what he wanted from witnesses by bullying anyway, had both these well in check, and with time even his brogue moderated noticeably. He soon began to make his mark a second time around, particularly in civil actions.

However the case which really attracted wide attention and made him a national name was criminal and involved his old Trinity College acquaintance Oscar Wilde, and Carson's part in this has sometimes been misrepresented. When Oscar Wilde took the rash step of prosecuting the Marquess of Queensberry for Criminal Libel over the accusation of homosexuality, a charge on which Queensberry could easily have been sent to prison, Carson was asked to defend Queensberry and after some hesitation he agreed to do so. In court Carson sparred with Wilde for some time, but when the over-confident witness made a slip Carson was ready; he asked Wilde if he had ever kissed a certain young man, and Wilde answered he had not, because "he was a very ugly boy". Carson spotted the implications in this unguarded reply and pounced—from then on he carried out the progressive unmasking of a sorry pervert with a taste for younger men way beneath him both socially and intellectually. Inevitably Queensberry was acquitted and Wilde then prosecuted, but Carson refused to have anything to do with this prosecution, feeling that to do so would seem vindictive.

This is perhaps his best known case, though it was only one of his very many important appearances in court. Not infrequently his opponent was another rising legal star of his generation, Sir Rufus Isaacs, and the gladiatorial contests between the two became a popular feature of the legal scene at a time when leading barristers had a considerable public following. Both were men of sufficient stature for this never to spill over into any personal animosity and they were always on good terms, though their backgrounds and political outlook differed greatly.

When the Conservatives came back to power after a short period of Liberal rule Carson was once again offered a Government post, a very unusual one for a former Irish Law Officer, Solicitor General of the United Kingdom, which brought with it a knighthood. He got this job despite not having always been a 'good party man' and even in Government maintained an independent approach as far as possible; all the time he made it quite clear that his only deep political interest was in Ireland. Then after the General Election of 1905 he was in opposition once again, and able to resume his regular practice at the bar.

A tall and somewhat dour looking man, Carson was undoubtedly one of the giants in a period which had its full share of outstanding men. By 1908, when he was 58, there was a good reason for everyone, including himself, to think he might shortly move into semi-retirement. He had never enjoyed the best of health, indeed he seems to have been a sickly person for much of his life, and he could be over-conscious of this to the point of hypochondria. However in the end he remained active at an age when many men are retired and died when he was over 80, so some of his ailments may have been an imagined exaggeration; or even a forensic trick to win a little extra sympathy for his client's case from the judge and jury.

He had married his wife Annette in his early working years in Dublin, and though their relationship had been very close at the start and she had nursed him devotedly through a serious illness, she had never quite managed to keep up with his development, and in later years they had grown somewhat apart. However around this time her health began to fail seriously and Carson realised in time just what she had meant to him and was able to repay her earlier devotion. Another domestic worry was that his and Annette's children, who were growing up, were giving, in various ways, cause for parental concern.

He allowed none of this to affect his work; as an advocate he always unhesitatingly pursued the interests of his clients and would never accept a brief which he could not believe in or carry out properly himself. He always eschewed the unhappy practice followed by some leading counsel of the day of farming out seemingly less important tasks to others. This is one reason why his services were sought by many of the wealthiest litigants who were prepared to pay substantial fees.

This was the man, one of the greatest and best-known lawyers of the day, whom Major Martin felt was the "one person" who could help his brother over the seemingly minor matter of the accusation of the theft of a five-shilling postal order. What Major Martin knew was that Carson was a dedicated lover of justice, and that if he could be convinced that a real injustice, even a small one, had been committed he would fight with as much determination as if he were a member of the family himself, and do it with all the immense skill and knowledge he had acquired in his years of legal practice.

The first task then was to persuade Carson. Major Martin knew him slightly as a leading figure in the Conservative Party and as they were both dedicated Unionists there was a mutual bind of political sympathy between them. However when Major Martin first raised the matter Carson was hesitant, and talked about thinking of retiring from the bar, but the persuasive Major managed to get him to agree to see the boy as a first step.

The Major then collected his brother—all this took place a day or two after George had left Osborne—and took him along to Carson's chambers. The boy was led along the Strand, into Fleet Street and under the arch which carries the ancient Prince Henry's Room nearly opposite the great Victorian Law Courts edifice where the matter was in due time to come to its climax, and down a small alley. Here immediately opposite the unusual round nave of the Temple Church stands Dr Johnson's Buildings, a clumsy grey Victorian office building. In Number 3 Carson had had his chambers since starting to practise in England.

The two entered a large, slightly musty office, which in the view of another lawyer, Sir John Simon, who visited it, was "not overstocked with legal books", and which would have purveyed at least a slightly oppressive atmosphere to anyone unaccustomed to this type of surroundings. The young boy must have wondered what was in store for him, though neither he nor his brother can have fully expected what was about to take place.

Carson said he wished to see George alone. He showed Major Martin into an ante-chamber separated from the main office only by a curtain so that he could hear all that was said. He instructed the Major firmly that he must stay there and not intervene whatever happened, or he would drop the case.

Then lawyer and boy faced each other.

At this moment Carson may have recalled an incident from his own schooldays which showed how easily a wrong accusation can be made. Some money had been stolen and for no particular reason one boy became the popular suspect, even to the point where, under pressure, he made a half-hearted confession. Carson had his doubts and persuaded the others to set up an enquiry. While this was going on he noticed that another boy kept looking at his boots; quickly he pointed this out and the boots were taken off. Inside them was the stolen money.

Carson started to question George. The boy's story was not too clear as he was still a bit uncertain why the Osborne authorities were so convinced he was the thief, but by patiently eliciting the various details Carson soon had a good idea what had happened. It helped him that he knew Osborne at first hand for his own son Walter had been a cadet there not so long before. If George was at times hazy about some matters he remained throughout adamant about his innocence. Sitting behind the curtain Major Martin heard Carson's still modest brogue dart the most leading of questions, suggesting that George was really the thief, he had taken the postal order for a joke perhaps and was now afraid to own up even to his own family, who so firmly believed in him and who were prepared to take so much trouble on his behalf.*

* My information on details of this event comes from Lieutenant-Colonel Jack Archer-Shee whose father, Major Martin, recounted the story to him. Unfortunately though Carson made a record of the examination I have been unable to trace it. Many Carson papers were destroyed when the Northern Ireland Public Record Office was bombed in the 1939–45 War.

Devotees of the Rattigan play will recognise this as the scene which provides the exciting end to the first act; however no attempt should be made to compare Carson with the fictional lawyer, Sir Robert Morton, clearly a very different character.

Carson had a remarkable ability to dominate a witness without seeming to bully them, and had the boy made a single slip under this ordeal there is no doubt he would have spotted it instantly, as he had with Oscar Wilde years before.

This all came through clearly to Major Martin sitting behind the curtain and several times he felt like intervening to protest against such treatment of his young brother, but he remembered what Carson had threatened would happen if he did. He steeled himself to listen passively, trusting that Carson was only doing what he felt was really necessary. Quite abruptly, after nearly three hours, his faith and patience were rewarded. The curtain was whisked aside.

"The boy is innocent," said Carson. "I will defend him."

5

LAWYERS GET BUSY

Carson had been very impressed by young George during this intensive session. The boy had stood up very well to the forceful examination and had not only convinced the lawyer that he was completely innocent, but also that he was of such character to be well worth defending. Even with his knowledge of the ways of government it is doubtful if Carson realised quite what a long struggle was in store, but whatever was to happen he was now prepared to march shoulder-to-shoulder with the Archer-Shees on any course which was necessary.

In addition to Carson, the barrister, a solicitor was also needed, for under the British legal system he is the essential go-between between barrister and client; he also carries out all the basic routine work and makes formal contact with other parties. Major Martin had a friend, Mr Reginald Poole, the junior partner in one of the leading firms of the day, Lewis & Lewis;* they had frequently briefed Carson who also knew them well and so they were a natural choice.

This firm had interesting origins. It had been founded in the reign of William IV by the father of the present senior partner, Sir George Lewis. When Sir George had first joined his father in the practice in mid-Victorian times the office in Holborn Bars might well have served as a model for one of Charles Dickens's law firms, though it was an established and successful business. It was when the founder died and his son took the full reins that it began to move into a position of pre-eminence.

* Today Penningtons & Lewis & Lewis of Lincoln's Inn Fields.

George Lewis made a public reputation by his handling of some important cases including a big City fraud and as a cross-examiner in the 'Bravo' inquest, one of the most extraordinary inquests ever held, in which what at first seemed an ordinary suicide case was shown to have the most dubious background. He also appeared before the Parnell Commission which investigated some letters that *The Times* had published which suggested that the Irish Nationalist leader Parnell was advocating violence; Lewis was instrumental in showing these to be forgeries, despite assurances by a handwriting expert, the familiar Mr Gurrin, that they were genuine; this earned him a knighthood.

However it was not in cases which had great publicity that George Lewis really made his name. His real accomplishments were in privately helping people of importance who found themselves in trouble. He acquired an immense knowledge of the seamy side of society and he combined with this a remarkable memory so he had to make very few notes. Among his clients were numbered members of the royal family, and he was a personal friend of King Edward VII. He was not a great lawyer in the strict sense of the term but he was the most distinguished member of his profession at the time.

Not everyone admired him, for he sometimes espoused the causes of people widely considered to be scoundrels. A friend told him once that he thought that in a certain case he had done the public no service. The reply Lewis gave was: "The public was not my client". Unfortunately for history Lewis destroyed all his papers before he died and eschewed writing any memoirs; such a document could have been a fascinating exposé of the underside of society life in late Victorian and Edwardian times.

By 1908 he was in semi-retirement, the day-to-day business of the firm was being run by the other partners, his son and Mr Poole, though he still stepped in on occasions of real importance. When Major Martin got in touch with Mr Poole, the firm immediately wrote to the Admiralty and requested permission to inspect the documents in the case "at the earliest possible date". This letter was sent on 20th October, the day after George left Osborne, which shows that no-one was wasting any time.

When it was received by the Admiralty there was some uncertainty what to do. From now on the matter was, for the most part, dealt with by civil servants, and the only member of the naval staff who had anything to do with it was the Second Sea Lord, Vice-Admiral Sir William May, whose responsibility was for naval personnel. A formal acknowledgement to the letter was sent immediately and then attempts were made to decide what to do next.

They soon knew that the Archer-Shees were being advised both by Sir George Lewis and Carson, and must have realised that a pair of fifteen-inch legal guns were being trained on them. The mixed emotions and uncertainty with which they dealt with the lawyers' requests are illustrated by the various notes attached. The letter went first to the Secretary, Sir Charles Thomas, who sent this note to the Treasury solicitor:

> Please advise me as to answer. The boy was not dismissed, but his father was requested to withdraw him. The Postal Order had been returned to Osborne Post Office, and as a general principle inspection of official papers by outside persons is to be deprecated.

The dubious argument that George "was not dismissed" from Osborne because his father had been requested to withdraw him was one the Admiralty was to advance on a number of occasions.

The answer from the Solicitor was inclined to be more helpful.

> The general principle is of course important and cannot be questioned. But I think there is a distinction between official reports and documents, and the evidence upon which the Admiralty have reached a decision of this kind. The consequences of a charge of this kind to the boy are of course extremely serious and I think, having regard to his age, that his father should be allowed to know the evidence against him. I fully realise that the most anxious steps are taken to reach a final conclusion, but to refuse to inform the father of the facts alleged would, I think, tend to produce a feeling of injustice. If this information is given it would enable the father to appreciate the wisdom of withdrawing the boy.

Sir Charles Thomas reacted to this:

> Concur with the Solicitor that it would be extremely questionable policy to withold the evidence from the father. If this is concurred in I propose to arrange an interview between Sir George Lewis and Lord Desart.

Lord Desart, as Treasury Solicitor, was an important and respected Government official. He was a member of the Irish Peerage who before entering the Law had spent a short spell in the Royal Navy, but had concluded his mind was more atuned to problems of legal analysis than maritime strategy. Soon after qualifying he had joined the office of the Treasury Solicitor and had risen there in 1894 to the top position. This at the time was actually a triptych of offices, Treasury Solicitor, Queen's Proctor and Director of Public Prosecutions. In 1908 however it had just been decided to hive off the last position and appoint a separate Director of Public Prosecutions so Lord Desart was now concentrating, in the last year before his retirement, on the work of Treasury Solicitor and the now named King's Proctor. The latter post involved intervening in divorce cases as a third party where he had information which might affect the court's decision and it was a task he always found unsatisfactory believing that it did more harm than good. As Treasury Solicitor he was responsible for providing, with the aid of a professional staff, a legal service for a number of government departments including the Admiralty. It was in this capacity that he was now involved. He was fully briefed about the events at Osborne and he then got in touch with Sir George Lewis to arrange a private meeting which was in effect to be a back-door attempt to squash the matter in its infancy.

It took place on 29th October, nine days after the first contact by Lewis & Lewis. Lord Desart laid down the basis of the meeting by telling Sir George that he had asked to see him this way because he knew anything he said would not be made use of as committing the Admiralty in any way. Sir George asked if he might tell Carson on the same understanding and Lord Desart readily assented, "knowing how worthy of confidence Sir Edward Carson was" as he reported to the Admiralty afterwards, and also, more cynically, because he considered that Carson was "the only person who was the least likely to be able to exercise any influence on the family".

Lord Desart then presented the facts as he had them to Sir George who replied that he already knew most of them, though he had assumed that the Osborne postmistress had identified George. He gave the impression to Lord Desart that he thought that the postmistress's evidence must be accepted, and if so then the case against George was really conclusive. However he explained that the family were determined to do everything they could to obtain some additional investigation and press the matter further. Lord Desart then suggested that such a course could do nothing but harm as it would create publicity, whereas if nothing more was said the knowledge of the affair would be limited to those who were present at Osborne. He seemed unaware how these things can stick to a person, and to have been "expelled from Osborne for stealing"—which despite all protestations about only having asked his father to withdraw him is how the matter would have been generally viewed—could have been a handicap to George for life.

Sir George showed Lord Desart a lengthy written statement which Carson had taken from George and which Lord Desart noted that

George Archer-Shee in his cadet uniform with his father

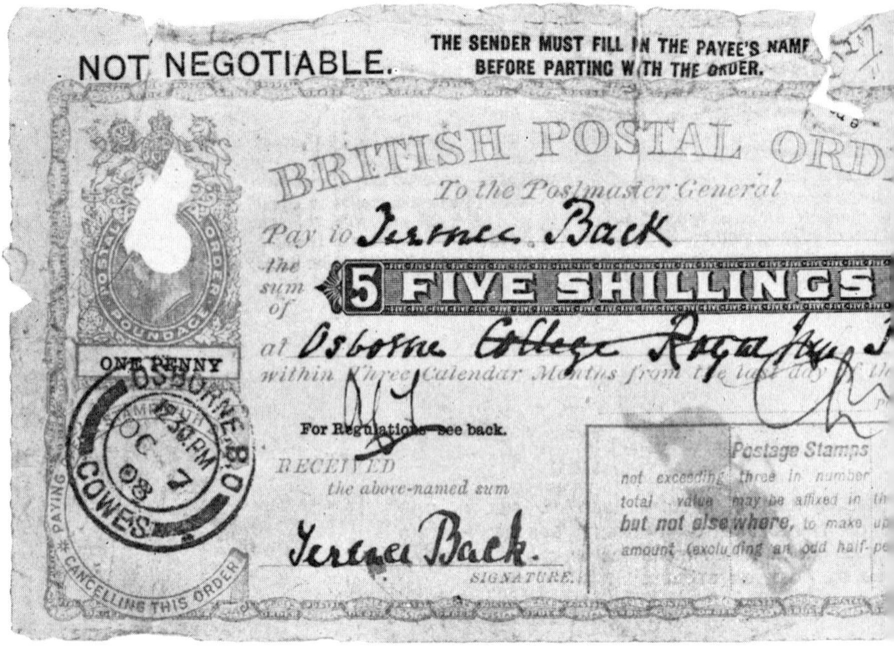

NOT NEGOTIABLE. THE SENDER MUST FILL IN THE PAYEE'S NAME BEFORE PARTING WITH THE ORDER.

BRITISH POSTAL ORD

To the Postmaster General

Pay to *Terence Back*

the sum of **5 FIVE SHILLINGS**

at *Osborne College Regatta*

within Three Calendar Months from the last day of the

For Regulations—see back.

RECEIVED the above-named sum

Terence Back.
SIGNATURE.

ONE PENNY

OSBORNE & COWES
OC 7 08

POSTAL ORDER — POUNDAGE
PAYING — CANCELLING THIS ORDER

Postage Stamps not exceeding three in number, total value may be affixed in th but not elsewhere, to make up amount (excluding an odd half-pe

NOT NEGOTIABLE. THE SENDER MUST FILL IN THE PAYEE'S NAME BEFORE PARTING WITH THE ORDER.

BRITISH POSTAL ORD

To the Postmaster General

Pay to *W. J. Bassett-Lowke C*

the sum of **15/6 FIFTEEN SHILLINGS & SIXPENCE**

at

within Three Calendar Months from the last day of t

For Regulations—see back.

RECEIVED the above-named sum

G. Archer-Shee
SIGNATURE

Three Half-Pence

POSTAL ORDER — POUNDAGE
PAYING OFFICE STAMP WITH DATE — CANCELLING THIS ORDER

...THAM
1.15 PM
OC 12 08

ONE PENNY   ONE PENNY

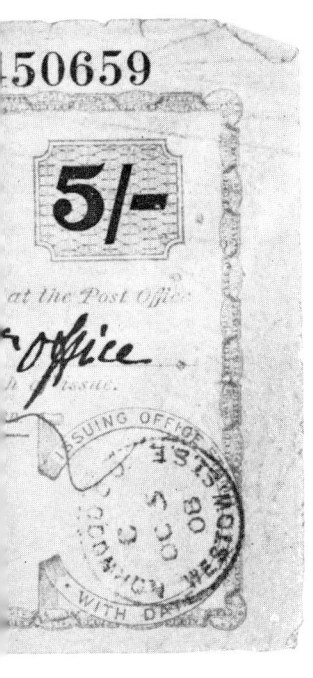

(*above left*) The stolen postal order and (*below left*) the postal order which George bought. (*above*) Osborne House showing the corner where the post office was situated

(*above left*) Commander R. G. A. W. Stapleton-Cotton MVO; (*right*) Captain
Arthur H. Christian MVO, ADC, RN

(*below*) A view of the reading rooms at Osborne

though it contained nothing but a denial of the theft, it was not, according to his recollection, inconsistent on material points with the information on which the Admiralty acted.

Sir George complained that he had not been allowed to see the handwriting on the stolen postal order, and said he thought he should have been shown this. The lofty reply he received was that the authorities were really the judges of what should be done, and could have no desire to do anything but justice. The meeting closed with Lord Desart under the impression he had succeeded in persuading Sir George that the best thing to do was to try and shut the Archer-Shees up.

Even if he had, and Sir George was far too canny and experienced to give anything unnecessary away, he totally misunderstood the Archer-Shees. Sir George said nothing which altered their determination, or Carson's, to press on with their demands for a full investigation.

Simultaneously a comedy of errors was taking place between the Admiralty and Lewis & Lewis; later the Admiralty were to suspect that this was part of a deliberate attempt to embarrass them by giving the appearance that they were being tardy. The day before Sir George Lewis met Lord Desart someone in Lewis & Lewis's office noticed that the letter to the Admiralty had not yet been answered. In view of the nature of the meeting, Sir George told no-one else in his office about it, and so his partners continued to pursue the normal courses of action. They wrote another letter to the Admiralty pointing out that it was ". . . a matter of so grave and urgent a character that we must ask you to let us have an answer if possible to our letter in the course of post".

Even after Sir George and Lord Desart met no-one else in the Lewis & Lewis office knew about it, but this was not appreciated at the Admiralty. They took no action, so after five more days Lewis & Lewis's tone became much curter. A hand-delivered note demanded "We should be obliged if you would inform the bearer, who will wait, whether we are to expect any answer to our several communications in this matter".

This provoked the Admiralty to telephone Sir George to enquire what was going on; had everything, they asked, been sorted out at the meeting with Lord Desart? Sir George reminded them of the terms of the meeting and explained that only he in his office knew of it; he added that they still wished to discover more about the evidence.

The firm sent a further letter two days later setting out in detail what they wanted to know. They asked for the post office to be requested to lend the postal order again so they could be shown it, and also to see the rest of the evidence; they also said they would like to go to Osborne to question witnesses, and to read the various reports on which the Admiralty had acted. The letter was taken to Whitehall by Mr Poole personally with a request that he be given an interview. Though a senior official did talk to him, what he said was very nebulous and led nowhere.

While all this was going on the original letter from Lewis & Lewis was still going around the Admiralty. When Lord Desart sent in his report on the meeting with Sir George Lewis he added the view that he did not consider the request to see the postal order unreasonable and suggested that it should be met, provided no official reports or documents were shown. It was on the request to see internal reports that Lewis & Lewis had touched the Admiralty on a very raw nerve. Lord Desart also recommended that Lewis & Lewis should be told that there was "other information quite apart from the handwriting which in the opinion of the Admiralty necessitated the removal of his son on the ground stated in the letter". This statement might have been calculated to make the Archer-Shees demand to know more.

An attempt to block even this modest proposal came from Sir William May, the Second Sea Lord. Earlier he had been in favour of showing the postal order, but now he had second thoughts.

> I am not in favour of the Action proposed by Treasury Solicitors. Sir George Lewis and Sir Edward Carson both now know all the evidence we have in support of the charge and we shall not gain any advantage in allowing Mr. Archer-Shee to see the Postal Order.

But McKenna, who had the final word, was prone to be a little more sympathetic.

> If by some miracle the boy could be proved innocent it would be a cause of great satisfaction to the Board. Although I fear such an event is impossible and that no purpose will be served by allowing Mr. Shee to see the Postal Order, still as he was made the request I think it should be complied with.

Just seeing the postal order was not going to be nearly enough for the Archer-Shees or their advisers. They now decided that their next step should be to make their own investigation at Osborne, with Mr Poole going there himself. This proposal was put to the Admiralty who concluded they could not really refuse, but they endeavoured to protect themselves by laying down a number of conditions. They demanded that Captain Christian should be given an advance list of all the college witnesses he wished to interrogate, and that all questions must be asked with the Captain present; the Captain also had the right to refuse to allow them to question anyone if he thought fit. In practice these limitations did not prove particularly inhibiting.

Miss Tucker and anyone else at the post office were not under Admiralty control; they were a matter for the postal authorities. Lewis & Lewis got in touch with Postal Headquarters where the view was taken that as one of their servants had been the key witness it was their duty to help all they could. They readily agreed to Miss Tucker and others being questioned, and sent instructions to co-operate to Osborne Post Office.

To finalise the arrangements for his visit Reginald Poole saw Sir Charles Thomas personally and told him he felt he would like the help of an experienced cross-examiner and asked if it would be in order to take a Mr George Elliot KC, a leading criminal lawyer, with him. Sir Charles agreed, and also told him that he had just heard that the postal order was now back at Osborne Post Office and he could see it there.

Mr Poole then got in touch with Mr Elliot and briefed him, and the pair were just ready to set out for the Isle of Wight when the Admiralty threw a spanner in the works. They now said they did not want Mr Elliot to question witnesses directly, but only through Mr Poole.

To this Poole and Elliot reacted immediately by cancelling their trip and lodging a furious protest. What was the point, they argued, of an experienced advocate going if he could not persue his normal function. Mr Poole also pointed out that after Sir Charles Thomas had told him the proposal to take Counsel was satisfactory he had immediately engaged and briefed Mr Elliot on this understanding. The Admiralty caved in under this onslaught and permitted Mr Elliot to question directly, adding a rider that both men went to Osborne "as friends of Mr Archer-Shee and not in any official capacity".

Eventually the two lawyers set out for the Isle of Wight on Monday 9th November, over a month after the theft had taken place. They spent a full day there talking to witnesses, came back to London to sort out their thoughts and then returned to the college nine days later to tie up loose ends. In all they questioned about twenty witnesses

—seven cadets, two college servants, CPO Paul, Gunner Gordon, Lieutenant Burrows, Commander Stapleton-Cotton and Captain Christian at the college, as well as three staff at the post office. Some of these contributed very little and one servant even told them this was the first he had heard of the matter.

The most interesting piece of completely new evidence they dug up arose out of the postal order George had sent to Bassett-Lowkes for his steam engine. The post office had lent them this and when they saw it two points struck them: the signature 'G. Archer-Shee' written at the bottom, and three penny stamps which had been stuck on, raising the value of the order to fifteen-and-ninepence. They asked George about these and he told them that he had been uncertain where to sign a postal order, and how he had asked about it in the reading room. On the stamps he was less helpful, and at first they presented a puzzle. George thought he might have stuck them on but as his engine cost only fifteen-and-sixpence there was no reason why he should have done so, and indeed if he had then a few pence were unaccounted.

This minor mystery proved to be a complete red herring and was quickly solved when Bassett-Lowkes were asked if they could shed any light on it. They explained that as they did a lot of business with schoolboys they often received payment for small orders in postage stamps. They got far more of these than they could use on their own outgoing mail and as the post office are only prepared to redeem unwanted stamps at a discount they had found they could get full value by sticking them onto postal orders they received before cashing them. This is perfectly legitimate and at that time up to three stamps with a total value of fivepence could be stuck on any postal order. Bassett-Lowkes checked their records and found that in the case of George's order they had done just this.

The signature however was of value and Patrick McNair was questioned about the scene in the reading room when George had written his letter. He clearly remembered George's uncertainty about the correct way to fill in a postal order and how he had openly discussed the problem, and that several cadets were present at the time. The lawyers took the view that it was clear from this that George did not properly understand postal orders, whereas the thief must have known all about them. They also felt his open behaviour was unlikely conduct for a thief.

There had been some implications that Terence Back had indicated he thought George might be the thief and so he was questioned with particular care. He was asked about all his movements with his postal order, and from his answers it was clear that quite a number of cadets knew that he had it and that around fifteen of them had seen him put it in his reading-room locker. He explained that he thought George was one of these, but when pressed about his supposed accusation of George he said that when reporting the theft he had recalled that George had gone to the post office that afternoon, but apart from this he had no other cause for suspicion.

When Cadet Arbuthnot was interrogated he confirmed what they already knew about his own visit to the post office, and added an interesting detail. He recalled that as he left the post office someone else, a college cadet servant, had passed him and gone in, though he had not noticed which servant it was.

The Admiralty had made much over the timing of George's visit. Miss Tucker had put it as a little over an hour after Arbuthnot had come in, which put it at about twenty past three. The timing of Arbuthnot's visit was confirmed by the despatch time of the telegrams Mr De Smit had sent while he was there and were noted as coming in at seven, eight and nine minutes past two. Arbuthnot must then have left about a quarter past two.

When first questioned at the college George was supposed to have said he had gone to the post office at half past three. The lawyers asked the boy for his own version of this and his recollection was that when asked about the time he had recalled the sentry bell and replied that it was "half past something". In answer to a question from the Captain whether it was half past three he had replied that it "might have been".

Some strong confirmation that it was much earlier came from telegraph boy Charles Langley at the post office. He remembered George coming in and he was certain it had been only a few minutes after Arbuthnot had gone out, certainly not nearly as long as an hour.

George's friend Patrick Scholes was also able to add that he clearly recalled George asking him at the flagstaff to accompany him to the post office. Scholes could fix the time quite accurately because it was shortly before his friends who took him out that afternoon had arrived, which had been at half past two. CPO Paul who had given George permission to go to the post office was uncertain about the time at which he had done this and could only recall that it was after Arbuthnot, but another cadet, Carmichael, had been nearly at the time and remembered it as being between two and two thirty.

Taking all this together there was considerable independent support for George's claim that the time was around half past two and that if Miss Tucker insisted it was later then in this respect she could be mistaken. However even besides all this there was Miss Tucker's main claim that the same boy who had bought the fifteen-and-six postal order had also cashed the five-shilling one. This, if true, was virtually unanswerable. It had of course been established that only one fifteen-and-six postal order had been sold at the post office that afternoon.

On their first visit to Osborne the lawyers did not get very far with Miss Tucker. The second time they went down she was not there, having come to London to visit friends for a holiday. The post office arranged for Poole and Elliot to see her at their headquarters next day and this time they elicited some interesting answers from her. No-one ever doubted her honesty or her genuine attempts to scratch her memory for the truth. She readily admitted that she had been totally unable to identify any of the cadets who had been put in front of her at Captain Christian's house and said that none of the faces she had seen at the parade there had brought back any recollection to her at all; she never paid much attention to those she was serving.

She agreed that she had told Gunner Gordon that she might be able to identify a voice, but when Captain Christian had interviewed the cadets so she could hear them speak she still utterly failed to recognise any of them despite trying her hardest to do so. She went even further and said that the voice of the boy who had cashed the postal order was different from any of those she had heard at the interrogation; it had "made less noise" and been "gruffer and thicker", and could have been the voice of a boy who had been running. No-one had suggested George had run to the post office so fast that he got out of breath and as he had permission to go there and was in no hurry there was no reason why he should have done so. The voice Miss Tucker describes could either have come from another cadet rushing on an illegal mission or from an older man.

Poole and Elliot also tested Miss Tucker's general recollection of events that afternoon. They asked how well she knew the cadet servants and she said that she saw some of them in the office quite often, particularly those who were pensioners and drew their money through her. However she had no memory of any of them coming in on the afternoon in question, though Arbuthnot had been certain that one had followed him in.

Despite all this on the one crucial fact, that the two postal orders had been cashed by the cadet who had bought one for fifteen-and-six she remained unshaken; an independent observer at her interrogation, a senior post office official there to 'watch over' what went on, noted how hard the two lawyers tried to move her on this, and that despite all their efforts they failed completely.

On the day before they talked to Miss Tucker in London, Poole and Elliot had an interesting conversation at Osborne Post Office with Miss Tucker's assistant there, Miss Barlow. Though she had not been in the post office at the time the postal order had been exchanged she had some useful information and ideas to offer. She recalled how Miss Tucker had told her the morning after the theft that she felt she would not know any of the cadets again as they all looked alike to her, and anyway she had not looked at the one concerned for long enough to recognise him again. Miss Barlow also had a plausible suggestion as to how the mix-up may have taken place in Miss Tucker's mind. The Osborne Post Office could be quite a busy place for one clerk on duty alone and she would have to divide her attention between the counter and the telegraph room behind. Arbuthnot's experience showed that ordinary business was sometimes interrupted for attention to a telegram. It was quite possible, Miss Barlow thought, that Miss Tucker had sold George his postal order and stamp, then been called into the telegraph room for a few moments and after she had finished there come out again to find another cadet or someone behind the counter and not realised they had changed over while she was gone: she may have confused the second figure with George.

This idea is not only an intelligent possibility but it came from someone who knew Miss Tucker and her work habits quite well. Miss Barlow would surely not have made it unless she thought from experience that Miss Tucker had the sort of mind that could be confused in this way.

Captain Christian and Commander Stapleton-Cotton also talked to the two lawyers at Osborne. The two officers admitted that similar thefts had taken place at the college quite frequently for some time, even before George entered there, and they had been worried about them. They discussed the break-in into George's till box which he had reported two days after the theft, and the lawyers asked if this had by any chance been part of a search for the two half-crowns: they were assured by the Captain and Commander that it was not.

Commander Stapleton-Cotton retorted that he had suspected that George himself was the culprit in an attempt to draw suspicion away from himself. The Commander explained that he suspected this because the hasp of the till in the box appeared to have been broken after the box had been opened; but the lawyers then carried out some experiments and showed that with a strong screwdriver it was quite possible to get a leverage on the box and force the lock, thereby breaking the hasp.

At Osborne the two lawyers also went over all the ground carefully. They noted in particular the siting of the post office and how easy it would be for someone to emerge from it, quickly vanish into some thick shrubbery and not be seen by anyone else coming in after them. They also had the postal order photographed. The college authorities checked on George's financial position which confirmed what they already knew, that he had not been short of money. Withdrawing the sixteen shillings from the college bank had reduced his credit balance from £2. 1s 0d to £1. 5s 0d and in addition to this he had over £4 in the Post Office Savings Bank.

Another bit of bureaucratic nonsense occurred when, after the second visit, Lewis & Lewis wrote to Captain Christian to ask for some details about the postal orders Arbuthnot had bought and cashed to see if this would help to fit a few more pieces into their jig-saw puzzle. The Captain sent the letter back smartly saying he could not deal with them directly and they must go through the Admiralty. They got the information they wanted, but after a few more days delay.

At some point Major Martin himself went down to Osborne unofficially, his purpose being to have a private talk with Commander Stapleton-Cotton. The Commander's elder brother, Lieutenant Wellington Stapleton-Cotton, had been a fellow officer of his in the 19th Hussars in South Africa, and Major Martin had been with Lieutenant Wellington when he was killed during the siege of Ladysmith. He used this friendship to obtain a discussion of the matter, but the Commander made it clear he was not prepared to accept that a mistake could have been made. The Major replied that then he could expect the matter to be fought to the bitter end.

At this time Mr Archer-Shee wrote to George's old headmaster at Stonyhurst, Father William Bodkin, who immediately rallied to his ex-pupil's side, something which was to have ramifications for his school later. Mr Archer-Shee asked for some character testimonials and Father Bodkin sent no fewer than seven from masters who had known George closely. His own view was that George was a "singularly honest and upright boy". Father Cassidy, from Hodder, had found him "honest and straightforward" and Father O'Neill, who had seen a lot of him at Stonyhurst, wrote:

> I can testify to his manly and straightforward upright and honest conduct on all occasions. I do not recall a boy of nicer character.

Mr Gordon Gorman, who was the navy class master, took a similar view.

> I always found him a gentlemanly boy, truthful frank honourable and studious, one of the best candidates I had for the navy for which I have been coaching for twenty-five years. I absolutely refuse to believe for a single moment he could be guilty of such a mean and contemptible act as the one of which he stands accused.

In addition Mr Archer-Shee prepared his own statement. This included a complaint about the lack of notification he had received while the matter was under initial investigation at Osborne and emphasised that the boy had "never given his parents a moment's anxiety as to his moral character". The father also reported that the family had received a great many letters from friends all containing indignant repudiation of the possibility of George committing such an act.

When all this information had been collated it was sent, together with complete records of the statements by the witnesses interviewed by Poole and Elliot, to Carson. He studied them all carefully and then produced an 'Opinion' which was a masterly summary of the case.

First he pinned the Admiralty's case against George to two points, the handwriting report and the statement by Miss Tucker. He dismissed the handwriting as being of little or no importance and said it was a class of evidence which no court would consider reliable. Miss Tucker, he suggested, could easily have been mistaken. He pointed out George's excellent character and while acknowledging that such a boy might be capable of giving way to an impulse if he was in need of money, it was quite clear from the bank statement that he was not. He considered it of the highest importance that there was no evidence that George had disposed of the two half-crowns, and indeed it was acknowledged that he had not used them for purchasing the postal order; he had already drawn sufficient money for this from the college bank and did not need any more. One point the Admiralty had made was that only two cadets had obtained permission that afternoon to go to the post office, and with a naive belief that authority would have been respected seemed to feel that this meant that no other cadet had done so. Carson pointed out that the reverse was the case and that a thief was much more likely to have gone stealthily than asked for leave.

He then analysed the possibility that the postmistress could have been mistaken; he pointed out her total failure to identify anyone and added that there was much more in her statements to suggest her recollection could be faulty, most notably the recollection of the telegraph boy that George had come into the post office soon after Arbuthnot. Adding all this up he asked:

> . . . how is it possible with any justice to brand as a thief and a forger a boy of 13 of the antecedents and character I have already described. It means disaster to him at the threshold of his life.

At Lewis & Lewis a lengthy letter was prepared covering every aspect of the matter. In eighteen typed foolscap pages all the relevant information which Poole and Elliot had obtained in their enquiries was examined and analysed and the basic argument that emerged was that they had unearthed enough new evidence to cast considerable doubt on George's guilt and consequently they urged that the question of what they referred to as George's "expulsion" be reopened.

To this they added Carson's Opinion, copies of all the statements which Poole and Elliot had taken, and copies of the testimonials received from Stonyhurst and Hodder; they also mentioned the letter George had received from his fellow cadets at Osborne. The bulky package went off to the Admiralty on 9th November, just over two weeks after Poole and Elliot had completed their investigation; in view of the paper work involved there must have been some intensive work to achieve this. The whole heavy meal was now for digestion by the Admiralty.

6

MR ACLAND ENQUIRES

At the Admiralty this was received and studied. It presented them with some difficulties, for the conclusion they drew was that while quite a number of holes had been punched in their case it had not been completely demolished. They did not feel that the arguments were strong enough for them to admit error and reverse their decision; apart from loss of face this would have meant showing lack of confidence in the authorities at Osborne, and also readmitting George with a shadow of doubt still hanging over him.

One of the minor consequences was that the Osborne authories were incensed when they learned of the 'Round Robin' letter sent to George. Those cadets of 'Drake' term responsible were called together by Lieutenant Burrows and soundly told off, a point he made in particular was that by signing with nicknames they had clearly regarded the matter far too lightly and so they would all be punished.* Mr Livesey was asked to account for his statement which found its way into the letter and he explained that what he had actually said was that he would not believe George was the thief until he saw satisfactory evidence. The whole civilian teaching staff at Osborne were annoyed by the way the matter had been handled by the naval side, they felt it was ham-handed and were irate at not having been consulted.

Lord Desart studied the papers and after some uncertainty passed

---

* Memories have, not surprisingly, become a bit confused over the years about the nature of this punishment. Two of the signatories both still vividly recall they were punished but one thinks they were "confined to the reading room" which meant being forbidden visits to the Tuck Shop or outdoor activities for a week, while the other thinks that the offence of sympathising with a term mate in trouble was considered to merit "corporal" attention.

them over to an outsider for a viewpoint; he sent them to the new first Director of Public Prosecutions, Sir Charles Matthews, whose experience he felt would be appropriate to give him some advice.

At the end of the term at Osborne Captain Christian came to London for a routine interview with Mr McKenna and they talked the matter over then. The upshot of all this was a decision to hold another enquiry, which would be conducted by the Judge Advocate of the Fleet, Mr Reginald Acland KC. The Judge Advocate is a civilian lawyer appointed by the Navy to oversee its justice. Normally his function is to study the reports of courts martial to check that the correct procedures have been followed and to act as a general critic of any new disciplinary proposals. It is not a full-time job: Mr Acland was also a practising barrister and Recorder of Oxford. When he was invited to undertake this enquiry Mr McKenna made it clear it was a special job, outside his normal duties.

Neither the Archer-Shees nor Lewis & Lewis were told of this decision immediately, and when about a week before Christmas they had heard nothing Lewis & Lewis wrote appealing for some news before the holiday, at least for George's sake.

Two days before Christmas the Admiralty replied briefly saying that they conceded the letter had unearthed new detail but they did not consider this put the matter in an entirely new light. They proposed to make further enquiries, but these could not take place until after the Christmas holidays; so at least George and his family enjoyed the season with a little hope.

Immediately after Christmas: Lewis & Lewis demanded to know if this meant the Christmas holidays at the Admiralty in London, or the much longer break at Osborne College; they also asked that George should be represented at this enquiry. The Admiralty replied that they meant the holidays at Osborne (which ended in the middle of January) and also that representation in the sense they meant "would not be appropriate". In other words the enquiry was to take place without anyone being present to represent George, and, most important, to question the witnesses on his behalf.

Meanwhile Major Martin was doing a little private investigating on his own. He contacted a friend in the post office, to whom he wrote that he knew his brother was not the thief "as certainly as I know my name", and obtained access to all the relevant Osborne Post Office records. In addition postal officials went to a great deal of trouble to trace the senders and recipients of all postal orders which had been through the Osborne office on the afternoon of the theft. Every piece of paper was combed for clues, in particular to try and identify everyone who had been into the post office that afternoon. Date stamps were also compared to see if the times of issue could reveal anything; the time of receipt by Miss Tucker of Mr De Smit's telegrams was also checked, though of course the post office were not prepared to show the actual telegrams themselves.

The most useful piece of new information turned up was a postal order which Cadet Servant Pritchard had bought that afternoon from Miss Tucker, whose initials were on it. Pritchard himself had acknowledged buying a postal order at about this time though when questioned he had not been quite certain on which day he had done so. Miss Tucker had said she could not recall him coming in and had been very uncertain if she had seen any servants at all that afternoon. This information was passed on to the Admiralty to try and show how poor Miss Tucker's memory could be; the big question always asked by George's friends was how could the good lady, who was so vague about most things, be so certain about the details of one particular transaction.

Mr Acland started his work a few days after Christmas by talking the matter over with Mr McKenna. Then he got in touch with Commander Stapleton-Cotton who was on leave in London and discussed with him the whole set-up at Osborne and the details of the system whereby a cadet had to get an initialled chit when he wanted to draw more than two shillings from the College bank.

He went down to Osborne as soon as term started there in the middle of January. He made extensive enquiries and talked to all those he thought could help him; whole notes were taken of what was said by a Mr Owen of the Treasury Solicitors Department.

Inevitably he first questioned Captain Christian, who now claimed that one thing that had made him suspicious of George was that the boy had at first admitted knowing that Back had received the postal order, and then later denied it. He also emphasised that cadets were not supposed to go into the reading rooms between two and three in the afternoon. George had never at any time denied this brief minor infraction of the rules which the college authorities seemed to think pointed so directly to his being guilty of the much graver charge.

Mr Acland made a thorough examination of all the territory concerned, the reading room and lockers, the dormitories and the post office and its surrounds. He inspected George's own chest in the dormitory to see how it had been forced, and he concluded that the hasp of the lock had been cut off with a file or small saw; he could find no marks on the edge of the till which he would have expected of it had been forced with a screwdriver or similar implement as Lewis & Lewis had suggested. He did not draw any really adverse conclusions from this; he could find no evidence that George had had any suitable instrument to make the cut and anyway he did not think that even a boy of George's age would think he could improve his position by what he called "such stupidity".

At the post office he questioned Miss Tucker with particular care. Once again she insisted that the boy who had cashed the stolen postal order was the same one who had bought one for fifteen-and-sixpence and some pressing would not move her an inch on this point. Mr Acland noted the "evident sorrow in her tone and manner" when she told him this. Her story had never varied now from the first, something which always impresses lawyers seeking a truthful witness. Miss Tucker also told him how the cadet she claimed had both bought and cashed a postal order had queried his change after the purchase and so she had checked in her drawer. This incident had also been recounted by George and to Mr Acland it helped show that Miss Tucker's memory was not as poor as had been suggested.

To check on the suggestion made by Miss Barlow that two people may have switched over while Miss Tucker was out of the office for a moment Mr Acland made an experiment; but before doing this he does not seem to have read the letter from Lewis & Lewis very carefully. They had said that Miss Barlow had suggested the switch-over could have taken place while Miss Tucker had been called into the room behind the main office to answer the telephone and deal with a telegram; Mr Acland experimented on the basis that the switch-over might have taken place while she just turned away for a moment to a table to date-stamp the postal order she had just received from the thief, and that while she was doing this he had left and George had come into the office. He concluded that this was most implausible as she would only have had her back turned for a few seconds and for almost all of the time she would have been able to see through the window up most of the long flight of iron steps which led down to the post office, and should have noticed anyone coming for some seconds before they entered. From the experiment he carried out his conclusion was the right one, but he did not deal properly with the suggestion Miss Barlow had made.

After talking to the telegraph boy Charles Langley he concluded that his evidence on details was worthless. During the afternoon in question Langley had had very little to do and so had sat rather inattentively in the corner; in one respect he bore Miss Tucker out: he confirmed that only two cadets had come in during the afternoon.

What made Mr Acland believe that Miss Tucker was right in her estimate of the time was his talk with Terence Back. Back recalled meeting George at the reading room door just after he had found the postal order missing. This had happened after he had been out 'pulling', as the navy calls rowing, and he estimated it to have been at about quarter to four, which fitted in with Miss Tucker's estimate, assuming George had gone straight from the post office to the reading room. There is no record that he ever actually claimed to have done this, and if he had by his own reckoning he should have got to the reading room well before three o'clock when it was still out of bounds. As he had found a number of other cadets there already this was most improbable.

Mr Acland discovered that the claim by Miss Tucker that all cadets in uniform tended to look very much alike to a stranger was confirmed by his own experience. He found that sometimes he could not recognise a cadet to whom he had been talking only the day before, and he thought this could easily happen with George whom he described as of a "common boyish type, an ordinary decent-looking gentleman's son". Though this explained Miss Tucker's failure to make any positive identification, it also makes more plausible the 'switch-over' explanation.

Mr Acland accepted the criticism of the original handwriting investigation, and so before he left Osborne he collected a sample from everyone who could possibly have been in any way involved; he got each one to write 'Terence Back'. He then returned to London and concluded this was not really adequate, so he got in touch with Lieutenant Burrows back at Osborne who had all the boys who had been in the reading room when George had come in to write out a sample sentence "Working in the Territorial Army would make Mr Brown's back ache". The whole sheaf of samples, 37 in all, were then sent to Mr Gurrin, including one supplied by George; they were numbered and Mr Acland carefully inserted George's near the middle, at number 16.

When Mr Acland had finished at Osborne he asked to see George. Major Martin and Mr Poole took the boy along to his chambers in the

Temple. As he went along there George was walking over familiar ground under an archway from the Strand, past Dr Johnson's Building where Carson had quizzed him so ruthlessly and across a courtyard to Hare Court, for another interrogation.

Mr Acland opened by telling George that he need not answer any questions unless he liked; Reginald Poole then assured Mr Acland that his parents were anxious he should answer anything he was asked. Mr Acland then started to question the boy in some detail, going over all the events on the afternoon of the theft. George made a favourable impression on the Judge Advocate on this occasion, who noted the "frank and clear way" he made his statement, looking his questioner straight in the face; the only reservation he had was that George seemed "a little too self-possessed".

Mr Acland also told Reginald Poole at this meeting how he had been told at Osborne that George had first admitted knowing Back had received the postal order and then denied it, a piece of evidence he felt was very important though it had not been mentioned before. Mr Poole admitted this was the first he had heard of it and said he would therefore like time to think about it. He asked for a copy of Mr Owen's notes to which Mr Acland agreed and they left after arranging to bring George back again the following afternoon. Major Martin, Mr Poole and George then went to dinner.

During this meal George began, for the first and only time throughout the whole series of events at which he was the centre, to show the strain of it all. Up to then his unworried attitude had impressed many of those who had talked to him but now it deserted him: at dinner he fainted.

He had not fully recovered when he was taken back to Mr Acland in Hare Court late the following afternoon; he was still looking pale and gave a very different impression from the day before. Mr Acland this time questioned him about his movements around the time of the theft and in particular his visit to the reading room where he said he had gone just to leave his money while he went to the dormitory to change. What puzzled Mr Acland was why he should have bothered to go to the reading room at all when there seemed no reason why he should not have taken the money along to the dormitory with him.*
George was not very clear about this himself and gave his answers in a

---

* The suggestion in the play that George had gone along to the reading room for an illegal smoke seems to be Rattigan's; the reading room was far too open a place for such clandestine activity.

way which contrasted markedly with his assurance on the previous day; he was now hesitant and Mr Acland felt he had been taken by surprise and he was not telling the truth.

When this was over Major Martin and Mr Poole were both concerned at what had happened, and after a moment's consultation Mr Poole went after Mr Acland whom he found coincidentally in the chambers of Sir Rufus Isaacs who was later to become very involved in the case himself. There Mr Poole told Mr Acland about George's faint the day before and how the boy was clearly now under considerable strain; he asked for the report to be delayed so they could consider their position and Mr Acland agreed to this. He knew that Mr McKenna was away from the country for a few days and so there would be no urgency anyway. The afternoon's events had however virtually damned George in his eyes and he was now almost certain that he was the thief.

If he needed any confirmation it came a few days later when Mr Gurrin made his report. The handwriting expert came along to Hare Court and Mr. Acland asked him which of the 37 numbered specimens he considered to be most like the signature on the postal order. Mr Gurrin pulled out number 16, George's.

It occurred to Mr Acland now that perhaps Mr Gurrin had recognised the writing from the earlier occasion when he had been shown it, but Mr Gurrin assured him that he had not the slightest idea he had seen any of the writings before. Mr Acland then told him that he had pointed the finger once again at George and Mr Gurrin replied that he could not be at all happy about this as his own son had been George's schoolmate at Stonyhurst.

Now Mr Acland drew up his report for Mr McKenna. He set out all the points he had investigated and endeavoured to answer the points which Lewis & Lewis had made in their letter. Most of them he dismissed, only acknowledging that George did have plenty of money in the bank at the crucial time and so had no need to steal, which he regarded as one of the inexplicable features of the case. He considered the point about George not knowing where to sign the postal order discounted because the boy told him he could not remember ever having sent a postal order away before. Many of his views he had formed from the impressions the witnesses made on him; he had questioned a number of cadet servants and said he found nothing in what they said or the way they said it to make him suspect any of them.

Finally, he concluded:

> Taking all the facts together it seems to me impossible to escape the
> conclusion that the Postmistress' story is correct and that the same boy
> changed the 5/- order as bought the 15/6 one, and that that boy is G.A.S.
>   R. B. Acland
>   January 25 1907

The whole report reads as if it was prepared in some hurry; ideas
are not presented in any obvious consecutive order. Mr Acland had
to apologise to Mr McKenna for the poor quality of the typing as the
typist had had some difficulty in reading his handwriting. When
dating it he was clearly confused by the new year, but went backward
rather than forward: it was now 1909.

When he received this Mr McKenna had no alternative and now
Lewis & Lewis were shortly informed that the original decision could
not be reconsidered. They were not given any additional information
or told about anything Mr Acland had unearthed; in many ways they
were more in the dark than ever. To make any further progress would
need considerable ingenuity and original thought.

THE PETITION
IS LAUNCHED

This seemed final but Lewis & Lewis made a few more desperate passing feints at the Admiralty even though they must have realised that the official mind was now firmly made up and most unlikely to be moved. They first sent in an enquiry asking what additional information the Admiralty now had which had led them to this decision, but got a curt refusal saying that the Admiralty had "nothing to add" to what they had already said. They then suggested that the matter should be considered by an independent arbiter and proposed the names of a few legal luminaries they felt might be suitable, but they got a similar answer.

This was early in February 1909 and meanwhile the Archer-Shees were preparing for an important change in their life as Mr Archer-Shee got ready to retire from the Bank of England; he was nearing his sixty-third birthday and at the very end of February would have been with the Bank for twenty-eight years. His health was giving him some trouble, no doubt the worry over the case was a considerable strain, and the Bank agreed to his retirement and gave him a pension. They all left Bristol and moved to a pleasant Gloucestershire village, Nailsworth. At the beginning of term George had gone back to Stonyhurst to continue his education; the school was still standing firmly by him, to the irritation of the Admiralty.

Faced now with a total refusal by the Admiralty to enter into any further discussions on the matter they were in some difficulty to know what to do next. The only possible remedy seemed to lie through the courts, but the law was not very helpful in giving them an opening.

They first considered trying to arrange for a prosecution which would have brought George into court where all the evidence would have been examined, and the witnesses subject to close scrutiny. They thought at first that this might be done either by persuading the Director of Public Prosecutions to bring a case, or by getting a group of friends to do so. Neither course proved practical. The Director of Public Prosecutions was not interested in helping—they could not know he was already familiar with the case as he had been consulted by Lord Desart—and a provate prosecution by friends could easily become an unconvincing farce if the Admiralty declined to cooperate, which seemed not unlikely.

When this idea had failed they turned their attention to civil courts to see if some way could be found to bring the matter here. In civil law there are two basic types of action, for tort—a corrupted ancient French word meaning a 'wrong'—or for breach of contract. A man who thinks he has been unfairly dismissed from a job may be able to bring an action under either, or sometimes both headings. If he were unjustly accused of theft he would probably allege a tort, while if some agreed procedure in his contract of employment had not been carried out he would sue for breach.

However those who work for the crown are in a rather special position. As an extension of the ancient principle "The King can do no Wrong", his servants in their official capacity can not normally be brought to court by another citizen. Specifically it has been ruled by the courts on a number of occasions that neither a civil servant nor an officer in the armed forces can sue for wrongful dismissal.

The Archer-Shees' lawyers, Carson and Lewis & Lewis, brought their considerable legal knowledge to bear to see if there was any way they could force the Admiralty into open court and make them present the evidence they claimed to possess. A difficulty they faced was that no-one had really decided what was the status of a cadet. Was he a servant of the Crown, civil or military, or just a schoolboy?

If he were a civil servant he would certainly have been brought to court, a civil servant suspected of theft is always prosecuted however minor the matter, and any naval officer is entitled to demand a court martial. As far as schoolboys are concerned the courts had ruled in the nineteenth century that a private school does not have arbitrary right of expulsion and they had been prepared to listen to cases brought before them. However it was hard to see if George had come under any of these categories, any likelihood that he could be considered a servant of the Crown was discounted by his not getting any pay, also the Admiralty had never indicated that cadets were subject to court martial. Osborne was not a private school even though it was run on similar lines to the established 'public' schools.

Eventually Carson alighted on a solution which, though it might not be good law in the strict sense, could have the effect of forcing the Admiralty into court. He recalled the ancient and somewhat unusual legal procedure known as 'Petition of Right' which is the only exception to the rule that the Crown cannot be sued. Under this a case can be brought for breaches of contract only under the theory that the Crown itself gives permission for this to be done.

The procedure is that a petition is drawn up setting out details of the alleged breach of contract and presented to the sovereign. If he accepts it he endorses it and the case can then go to the courts in the normal way. Though of very ancient origins the practice had been formalised fifty years before by The Petitions of Right Act, 1860, which made no fundamental change in the cases where such a petition might or might not be used, but set out the procedure for both submitting such a petition and for its hearing in some detail; it also made provisions for the payment of the costs of such cases which were basically similar to those in any other civil action. It also laid down fairly tight time schedules for both sides to follow once the endorsed petition had been presented, which would prevent either side pro-crastinating.

As George was a minor there could be no question of his petitioning himself; his father would have to act on his behalf. The basic argument that Carson had worked out was that the Admiralty was in breach of an agreement with Mr Archer-Shee to educate his son for the Royal Navy.

The petition on these lines was then drawn up.* It consisted of five foolscap pages much of which was devoted to quoting from the relevant Admiralty Regulations and the documents which Mr Archer-Shee had signed when he had applied for George to go to Osborne. In flowery legal language it recalled that it had been "mutually agreed between Your Suppliant and the Commissioners for executing the office of the Lord High Admiral of the United Kingdom of Great Britain and Ireland (hereinafter called the Admiralty) acting on behalf

* Appendix I.

of Your Majesty that in consideration of Your Suppliant undertaking to make certain annual payments his subject should, subject to the regulations then in force, be admitted to the Royal Naval College at Osborne and there trained as a Naval Cadet with a view to his entering in due course your Majesty's Navy". The fact that Mr Archer-Shee had made payments, and that if George had refused to enter the Navy at the end of his training the Admiralty would have claimed compensation from his father, was a strong point in support of their argument.

The petition claimed that the charge of theft made against George was "totally devoid of any foundation whatever" and that the boy's name had been permanently injured and his prospects in life greatly impaired by it. It concluded with a request that "his Majesty would be pleased to declare" that George had not stolen the postal order and the request for him to be withdrawn from Osborne was in breach of agreement.

The work of preparing this took a couple of months, and it was the middle of May before it was ready and printed. The main copy was then signed by Carson, and his junior Mr Leslie Scott, and in accordance with the procedure laid down in the 1860 Act, sent along to the Home Office. The Home Secretary at the time was Mr Herbert Gladstone, son of the great Victorian Liberal leader, but for him and his department the task in dealing with the document was mostly formal.

They first told the Admiralty about the petition, and asked for details about the case. The Admiralty replied with a summary and the observation that it was questionable whether this sort of matter should be dealt with by the courts. Internally they expressed the view that if this happened then they might have to institute courts martial for cadets, which they did not want.

These papers were then placed before the man whose task it was to advise the Sovereign whether or not to endorse the petition, the Attorney General. At this time he was a little-remembered holder of the Office, Sir William Robson, a personally popular man even among those who detested his strongly radical politics. When he had studied the papers he concluded that there was sufficient cause to advise that the petition should be endorsed, or possibly that he could find no good reason for not giving this advice. Though in theory endorsing a petition is entirely discretionary, in practice it is not refused when a sensible case has been made out, and had he advised against, Sir William could have been questioned in the House of Commons about it. However he gave a favourable view and in due course King Edward

VII wrote across the top left hand corner of the front page the striking traditional formula that meant proceedings could go ahead: "Let Right be Done". He added his signature "Edward R & I".

This took up a little more time, and it was about three months before the petition was returned, in the middle of August. Then the Archer-Shees' lawyers inscribed on it, as laid down by the 1860 Act, a formal request, called a 'prayer', asking for a plea or answer within twenty-eight days and it was sent along to the Law Courts Offices of the Treasury Solicitor. He promptly notified the Admiralty and they replied with a direct that the petition was to be defended.

However they soon had to take a much harder look at the matter and their counsel, Mr Cohen, was asked for an opinion. He replied that while he expected that the litigants would probably try to force the matter as a trial of the facts, that is whether George had stolen the postal order or not, he did not think the Admiralty should necessarily allow this, and should challenge whether or not there was any case in law. He said this depended to some extent on what the formal position of a cadet was, something the Admiralty now realised had never been properly resolved. On the facts he expressed reservations, saying that a jury's verdict would depend very much on the impressions made by witnesses.

The Treasury Solicitors decided that they wanted to go to the top for a decision whether or not they should submit what is known as a 'demurrer', a plea that such a petition did not lie in this case and the court could not hear it. This would have to be filed within the stipulated twenty-eight days which presented a practical problem, Sir William Robson whom they wanted to give the advice was particularly busy at the time.

The Liberal Government was currently trying to get through Parliament its notorious finance bill. This had included a number of Mr Lloyd-George's highly controversial social service and tax provisions which would never have been passed by the House of Lords as a separate measure; Lloyd-George had hoped that the tradition that the Lords would never throw out a finance bill would be continued, but the Peers of the Realm had disappointed him. Now, in an extraordinary constitutional situation, the Commons was examining the measure line by line, and Sir William had to be in constant attendance at the House to give legal advice. The long hours he spent sitting on the Commons Front Bench was much appreciated by Government supporters, though it meant he had little time to spare for other matters.

Before he was prepared to give the advice he was asked for he wanted to read all the papers.

So the Treasury Solicitors, the matter was mainly to be dealt with by Mr A. T. Hare who was head of the Law Courts Branch, asked Lewis & Lewis for 'extra time'. Though a timetable for the various stages was laid down this could be extended by agreement between the two sides, or if one side would not agree to a request the other could then apply to a Judge and have the matter argued out in front of him. To this request Lewis & Lewis replied that as the matter had been so long delayed they could not agree to more than a fortnight's extension.

Sir William now managed to find time to look at the papers and when the answer was filed it showed that the Admiralty were prepared to challenge the petition in both possible directions, in both law and fact. They would contend that there was no case in law for them to answer and that anyway even if there was they were right in what they had done, George had stolen the postal order and they had investigated the matter correctly and thoroughly.

The next step was for Lewis & Lewis to file their answer to this, for which they allowed a month. They were not quite ready in time and the Admiralty, despite the reluctance their own request for extra time had been granted, readily agreed to two extension of ten days. By now it was Christmas. Toing and froing between lawyers went on for some time. The Admiralty provided detailed plans of Osborne and the post office, charging the appropriate few shillings for each document and then the two sides decided to 'agree correspondence', which meant that a bundle of all the letters which had passed between them and other documents which they wanted the court to consider were put together and both sides examined them, and when they were happy that they were correct they agreed to accept them. When this was done the bundle contained no fewer than 169 pages, starting with the letter to George's father requesting George's withdrawal.

It was around Easter 1910 when it looked as if both sides would be ready to go to court, but then Lewis & Lewis approached the Treasury Solicitors asking for the matter to be ' stood over the vacation" which meant the court would not hear it until after Whitsun. It is not completely clear why all these delays were now occurring, but it seems probable that at least one explanation was that many of those concerned had other pressing political calls on their time.

Around this time Major Martin heard that there had been another, not dissimilar incident at Osborne a few terms before George arrived there. He got in touch with a Mr Harris of Yelverton in Devon who confirmed that his own son had been sent away from the College. It seems that during the holidays a Cadet Gabriel had cashed a postal order which had been taken at the college from another cadet. When asked about this Gabriel had insisted that Harris had given it to him, and the subsequent enquiry concluded that this story was probably true, and that at least there was enough doubt hanging over Harris for it to be unwise for him to continue to train for the Royal Navy.

When Mr Harris heard this he threatened legal action, and as a result Gabriel confessed that he was the thief. As all this had happened before George arrived it clearly had no direct bearing on the case, but does highlight the authorities' attitude in such matters. Mr Harris told Major Martin that he did not want the matter reopened, or even mentioned, and so nothing more was heard about it.

By early summer both sides were ready, and the case looked like coming to court before too long. Mr Archer-Shee wrote to the headmaster at Stonyhurst warning him that George might be called away at any time and expressing a little concern about the way the boy would face the rigorous cross-examination which was expected. George's school career had continued at Stonyhurst without incident, and few of the other boys there had known much about what had happened to him at Osborne.

Indeed up to this point few apart from those directly concerned had any idea what was going on. Nothing had appeared in press, nor had any questions yet been asked in Parliament; from the moment the petition had been presented the matter would have been *sub judice* and so no comment would have been possible. The British people were only now to learn something of what had been going on and what was to come, on the first explosive day in court.

8

POLITICAL INTERLUDE

The period when all this was taking place was one of the most politically contentious in Britain this century, and since a number of those involved were directly concerned it is worth while to remember what were the major issues of the day. The Liberal Government had marched into office in 1905 with many reforms and experiments it wanted to put into practice; but the defeated Conservatives, who still felt something of their traditional belief in a divine right to rule, saw almost revolution in many of these proposals and made it clear they were not going to give an inch more than they had to. They had one weapon up their sleeves, the House of Lords, who still had the right to reject outright any bill passed by the Commons. The Tory leader, Mr A. J. Balfour, made it clear soon after he found himself in opposition that he would not hesitate to get his noble supporters to use their power whenever he felt it was necessary, which led to Lloyd-George's famous jibe that the Lords were merely "Mr. Balfour's poodle".

One of the new Government's first major pieces of legislation had been a Trades Disputes Act designed to overturn a recent court ruling, the Taff Vale judgment, which had allowed an employer to collect damages from a striking union. Now unions were to be virtually immune from claims for damages, and surprisingly the Lords allowed this to pass. But next the Peers were sent an Educational Reform Bill and a Licensing Laws Bill, both of which they altered so much that by the time they were returned to the Commons they were emasculated and virtually unrecognisable. The Liberals, and the handful of Labour party sympathisers who worked closely with them, were furious, and made dark mutterings about the Lords thwarting the will of the people.

All this produced an agitated acrimonious atmosphere in national life. The radical-minded who saw their dreams thwarted, or not working out as they had hoped, became bitter, while Conservatives viewed developments with fear and anger. The Royal Navy managed to get itself near to the eye of this storm. A growing German Navy, rebuilt by Tirpitz at the end of the nineteenth century, posed a challenge to Britain's traditional position as ruler of the waves, and created demands for a substantial improvement in both the quality and quantity of Britain's fleet. The Navy League, which had been founded at the time when Tirpitz became active, led these demands, mainly with the slogan "We want eight, and we won't wait", referring to the most modern of battleships, the Dreadnoughts, which had been Fisher's brainchild. Other naval developments, including the Selbourne scheme and Osborne, had also attracted much critical comment.

Many of these arguments took place within the Royal Navy itself. Fisher had made too many enemies among other officers and had handled those who opposed his ideas too roughly to be popular everywhere; the situation had arisen among the more senior members of the service that they were either 'in the fishpond' and the limelight shone on them, or out of it on the bank and of little importance.

When the Liberal administration had come into office it had looked as if they would not give way to the more expensive naval demands, mainly for economic reasons; Lloyd-George, Chancellor of the Exchequer, was particularly anxious to have as much money as he could for his planned welfare innovations. However when McKenna arrived at the Admiralty he, at least, began to appreciate that the German threat was a serious one. Fisher, at this time First Lord, did not initially welcome the McKenna appointment. It is said he would have preferred a peer, a real Lord, in the job, but soon he began to realise that here was a man with whom he saw eye to eye on many things: a close bond sprang up and they worked together in harmony.

Sniping at this regime from both within and outside the Navy was common. The *Morning Post*, the leader of Conservative thought under its editor Fabian Ware, took the lead and could find little good to say about the way the service was being run, while in *Blackwood's Magazine* a senior serving officer, Admiral Custance, was allowed to give vent to vitriolic criticisms of the Admiralty under a thinly disguised anonymity. The Selbourne scheme and Osborne were often the targets of these critics who complained about the type of education offered, the health of the cadets and their accommodation, which they described as being in stables. It was true that the Royal Stables had formed the nucleus of the buildings, but most of them had been specially built, albeit in a rather temporary way.

A feature that was clearly disliked in some circles was the attempt to equate engineering with the regular profession of seamen officer. It caused great concern in upper-class households that 'gentlemen's' sons might find themselves forced willy-nilly into the dirty world of machinery. Despite this the number of applications for entry were always good—over 400 had competed for the 60 vacancies when George had sat his exam—even if many parents felt that Osborne was an evil they would have to tolerate to get their sons the career they wanted.

To some extent the Admiralty became over thick-skinned to these criticisms, and even when they were justified took little notice. The regime at Osborne was definitely on the tough side for such young boys, with a great deal of moving about 'at the double', and health problems were not uncommon. In Engineering Classes cadets often concentrated on doing just badly enough to avoid being sent to that branch, but not so badly that they were sent away from the college altogether.

The Admiralty's chief critic from within the service was a senior officer who had for some years been a bitter opponent of Fisher, Admiral Lord Charles Beresford. 'Charlie B' as he was known was virtually the last of a long line of naval officers of a type who would be considered unthinkable today, for he had combined an active and successful sea career with being a politician. He had sat for long periods in the House of Commons. He was the son of a noble Irish Protestant churchman, the Marquess of Waterford, who decided that two disturbing traits which he observed in his second son, Charles—a delicate disposition and an unwillingness to submit to parental discipline—would best be cured by the Navy. After a hesitant start Beresford took to life at sea; the Navy he entered still used sail as the main means of moving its ships, and early in his career Beresford had to witness the punishment of seamen flogged with the 'cat'.

He had just established himself in the service and was only a lieutenant when he was persuaded to stand for Parliament in his home area of the County of Waterford. His main platform was as an 'anti-Home Ruler' or Unionist and thanks to the efforts of his elder brother he won easily. From then on his career was a strange mixture of the Royal Navy and the House of Commons and in the latter he was never afraid to criticise the former; when on one occasion the Admiralty tried to prevent him from doing so Parliament firmly stood by the overriding privilege of Members.

In 1907, when he was sixty and out of Parliament, Beresford had been appointed Commander-in-Chief, Channel Fleet, an important appointment he would normally have expected to hold for three years; in giving it to him the Admiralty may have had at the back of their minds the thought that it would keep him away from making himself too much of a nuisance to them on the political front. However the appointment proved a stormy one, with several major rows, the best-remembered being Sir Percy Scott's notorious "paintwork before gunnery" signal; after this Fisher refused to order Scott to haul down his flag, to Beresford's fury.

Prematurely in 1909 Beresford's appointment was terminated, but to prevent him feeling it was too much a slap in the face, the post of Commander-in-Chief, Channel Fleet was itself abolished. Nevertheless Beresford immediately went into action against Fisher and the Board of Admiralty, and he did this with such skill, and so little obvious bitterness, that the Government was forced to sit up and take notice. He sent the Prime Minister, Asquith, a lengthy letter the gist of which was that the fleet was dispersed in such a way that if war came quickly it would take far too long to get it organised for hostilities.

Asquith replied that such allegations coming from an officer of his distinction would have to be looked into, and he set up a committee which he himself chaired to do just this. It is hard to say if the outcome was a victory for either Beresford or Fisher: Beresford's main contentions were rejected but not everything that came out about Fisher looked well, in particular his attempts to get officers on Beresford's staff virtually to spy on their chief. He left office at the end of the year; his successor was Sir Arthur Wilson, a far less effective or controversial holder of the position.

To sum up, the Royal Navy was the centre of much argument at the time. The deep traditionalists disliked almost every change which was taking place, and though Beresford was no reactionary his feuding gave these elements considerable comfort. Underlying all this was the real fear of the growing German Navy, and in retrospect Britain can be very grateful to McKenna for taking this seriously when many of his colleagues in the Government would have preferred to pretend it was not there. McKenna's skill in presenting his arguments in Cabinet was considerable and mostly he got the service what it required.

Chief of this opponents was Lloyd-George who had brought the whole national political ferment to a crisis by his 1909 Budget. It had long been an accepted custom that the one thing the Lords could not do was to reject a money bill, though in the absence of any written British Constitution there was nothing in practice to prevent them doing this. In his budget Lloyd-George had to find a lot of money, mainly because of the heavy demands of the Navy and Army and also to finance the newly-introduced old age pensions; he proposed to do this by taxing many of the most entrenched interests who had spokesmen in the lords, the landed gentry, coal and mineral royalties, and the liquor trade. To what extent he was deliberately setting out to provoke the Lords into taking the unheard-of step of rejecting a money bill is still a moot point, but whatever may have been in his mind this is what they did.

This provoked a genuine 'constitutional crisis', and the Prime Minister had no alternative but to dissolve Parliament and call a General Election, which was fixed for 15th January 1910. In those days there were no opinion polls so it was much harder to estimate a Government's standing and prospects, but there had been signs, particularly at some by-elections, that the Liberals were way past the peak of their popularity, and were going to have to put up a stiff fight to hold onto power. Asquith made it clear that, if they were returned to office, they would ask the King to create a sufficient number of sympathetic peers to pass the Budget and other Liberal measures, a proposal referred to by his opponents as 'packing' the House of Lords.

The election campaign gave Major Martin his chance. He was now formally nominated as Conservative and Unionist candidate for the constituency of Finsbury. This was a much smaller area than today with about 8,000 voters (all men of course) who in the main may best be described as prosperous working class. A large number in and around the Clerkenwell part of the area were jewellers and watchmakers which led to the district being called the workshop for the West End. In 1905 they had turned to the emerging Labour party and sent to Westminster the Secretary of the Bargemakers Union, Mr W. C. Steadman, a solidly orthodox working-class politician, proud to be a pillar of society and justice of the peace; in 1910 he was running again.

Despite their defeat in 1905 the local Tories were extremely well organised, under an able agent, Mr E. J. Wilkins. The constituency party had over a thousand members ready to play an active part, and in addition the younger generation in the Junior Imperial League formed a useful cycle corps of messengers to carry literature and messages. One of the awkward points they had to contend with was that by a historical anomaly a small part of the constituency in the Muswell Area was separated from the rest by several miles; at some point in time the Knights of St John, who had their headquarters in Finsbury, had had the right to gather wood in Muswell forest, and this had been preserved when Parliamentary boundaries had been drawn.

The General Election of January 1910, the first of two that year, was bitterly fought. The radicals and reformers, not at all certain of their future, were prepared to go to extreme lengths to try and hold onto power and many Conservative candidates were having great difficulties in putting their case across because of vocal rowdies trying to break up meetings. In the pre-radio and television era such meetings were the main way a candidate could make himself known and Major Martin realised that many of these toughs—the ancestors of today's 'Renta-crowd'—were moving around from place to place causing trouble in various constituencies where they had little connection. To overcome this he instituted a system of admission by ticket to all his meetings, tickets which were available impartially to any voter on the Finsbury Role irrespective of his political views, but not to outsiders.

This proved most effective in preventing trouble and allowing the Major to present his platform effectively. The two main planks of this were opposition to unrestricted free trade and demands for a large Navy (on which he would probably have seen eye-to-eye with McKenna). He was also ready to do battle for the Irish Unionist cause but this was not of great concern to the voters of Finsbury. What did worry them were the consequences of the Liberals' Free Trade policies, and the artisans of Clerkenwell in particular had felt the effects of an influx of low-priced Continental goods, produced by cheap labour, selling in direct competition to their own wares.

When after the end of voting on 15th January the ballot papers were counted the result was:

> Archer-Shee   3559
> Steadman   3187

So now he was Major Martin Archer-Shee, MP. The new position did not have any direct bearing on his brother's case, and in fact Major Martin never made any public utterances on the matter, either inside or outside Parliament, though doubtless he used his new opportunity to explain the matter to sympathetic fellow members in the smoking room of the House of Commons. When the matter did get to the floor of the Commons he left it entirely to others. Also returned to Parliament at this election were Sir Edward Carson, who easily held his Trinity College seat, and Lord Charles Beresford, who stood in Portsmouth, where his naval popularity helped him to an easy victory.

When the results from all over Britain were in, it was clear that the Liberals had suffered the not unexpected loss of a substantial number of seats. They now had a majority of exactly two over the Conservatives, with about eighty Irish Nationalists and forty Labour members in between. Even with Labour support for the Government the National-ists held the balance of power, and the question now was how far Asquith would be prepared to go to meet their demands over Ireland in return for their support for his radical measures, to which the Nationalists were not very sympathetic in principal. The answer, he soon revealed, was that he was prepared to go a long way, a lot further than he had indicated in any pre-election statement. In return for Nationalist support for the Government in the Commons Ireland would get a substantial measure of home rule.

In agreeing to this Asquith forgot the Unionists and Ulster. They saw in his moves, not without reason, one of the shabbiest political deals ever in British politics. Ulster in particular was outraged; this north-eastern part of the country has long been the awkward squad on the Irish scene; the people there are largely Protestants whose ancestors arrived from England in the seventeenth century and who have a bitter hatred of Roman Catholicism and a strong fear of rule from Dublin. They were prepared to fight in any way they could to hold onto the existing position, and in view of the way Asquith had made his arrangements they were prepared to be at least as unscrupu-lous.

The Unionists had their own committee at Westminster, and after the General Election the Chairmanship of this fell vacant. Carson was invited to take the post, and after a little hesitation he took what was probably the most important political decision of his career and accepted. He now became the champion of all the Irish who wished to remain tied to the United Kingdom, and in the bitter fight that was just starting, the leader of Ulster. Though not an Ulsterman himself, be became, as so often seems to happen in Irish politics, the outsider who espoused the cause with almost excessive vigour.

The first sign of what was brewing came in April when the new Home Secretary, Winston Churchill, made the Government's intentions clear in a Commons debate. That the statement should come from Churchill caused particular fury; he was already widely unpopular as a turncoat from the Tories and a 'traitor to his class', and now it was recalled that during earlier attempts to give Ireland Home Rule it was his father, Lord Randolph Churchill, who had coined the phrase "Ulster will fight and Ulster will be Right".

A blazing Parliamentary row took place in which Carson joined with genuine fury, he felt deeply that all decency had gone from public life with the Liberals' behaviour, and everything was still simmering near the boil when the Commons went into recess late in April. The nation then received an unexpected shock early in May, which poured at least a temporary cooling douche on national life.

The first indication came with an announcement that the health of the King "was giving cause for concern". By some standards Edward VII was a playboy, but in his own way he was very conscious of his duty and responsibilities and the political strife in the country had been a great worry to him for the past year or more, in particular because it was clear that despite his limited Constitutional position there was a good chance that he might have to become directly involved: if Mr Asquith persisted with his proposal to ask for the creation of a large number of peers who would support the Government then the King would have to handle the request, and there was no precedent to guide him. He had already indicated to Asquith that before he was prepared to consent he would require a further general Election.

It was clear to those close to him that he was seriously ill, though he was doing his best to fight it off and ignore it. On the morning of 6th May, against firm doctors' advice and despite admitting that he was "feeling wretched" he got out of bed to hold an important audience. However before the day was out he had collapsed and was taken to bed in a semi-conscious state. He was dead before midnight.

The brief Edwardian age now came to a close; the monarch who had inspired it despite, or because of his personal shortcomings had been immensely popular, and never has the death of a British king been greeted with a greater burst of national grief. He had provided a welcome reaction to the formidable personality of his mother and his efforts as a peacemaker were widely hailed at the time, even if they did not have very permanent results. At the time public talk was as if he had been the finest king ever to sit on the British throne; there was to be a reaction against this after a few years, particularly when a highly critical biography by Sir Sidney Lee appeared in the *Dictionary of National Biography*, but a long-range assessment is that in many ways he served his nation very well.

To return to the events which concerned young George Archer-Shee, these took place against a background in which acrimony between Government and Opposition had never been so bitter, and often spilled outside the Palace of Westminster. Former good friends ceased to be on speaking terms, and though the genuine motives of neither the Archer-Shee family nor Carson can be in doubt—Carson could not have had any idea how far the matter would go when he first agreed to become involved—there were others who would welcome any stick with which to beat the Admiralty and the Government. Events in the Law Courts that July were to give them a golden opportunity.

9
"LET RIGHT BE DONE"!

Almost exactly a year and nine months after the theft, on Tuesday 12th July 1910, the King's Bench Division of the High Court was ready to hear the case. The Judge was Mr Justice Ridley and representing George, or to be strictly accurate representing his father who was the formal petitioner, was of course Carson. He had the assistance of Mr Leslie Scott, KC, and Mr Eric Hoffgaard.

The Admiralty, or the Crown, which was the formal defendant, considered the matter so important that the second Law Officer, Sir Rufus Isaacs, led for their side. He was assisted by Mr Horace Avory, KC, and by Mr B. Cohen, who had advised the Admiralty in the early stages of the petition.

This then was to be another Carson and Isaacs clash, something which had become quite a common spectacle in the courts in recent years. They were two of the leading barristers of their day in their fields and had been briefed for opposite sides on many occasions.

Isaacs came from a very different background to Carson: he was the second son and one of nine children of a London Jewish fruit merchant, and he had to overcome a row of handicaps to rise to legal heights. That he had done so, and that other members of his family also achieved important positions is considered to have been due mainly to the influence of his remarkable mother, who guided her children most astutely. In the climate of the time, being a Jew was undoubtedly one of the handicaps.

Rufus Isaacs had finished his formal education at fourteen and then there had been thoughts of his making his career at sea with the

Merchant Navy. There is a legend that he ran away to sea but the facts seem to be that his parents planned to have him taken on as an apprentice, but when Rufus himself read through the articles of apprenticeship he decided he did not want to commit himself to something unknown for as long as the specified period of two years. Instead he signed on as ship's boy for a voyage to South America and when this was over he concluded the sea was not the life for him.

He then tried high finance and jointed the Stock Exchange as a jobber, but this came to disaster after a few years when he was 'hammered'. It was his mother who now steered him towards the law and after some study he soon established himself as an advocate, thanks to his good appearance, commanding voice and shrewd brain. His Stock Exchange experience now paid some dividend after the establishment of the commercial court in 1895 for he was one of the few men at the Bar who had such first-hand knowledge.

He also had political interests and as he was a radical by nature he joined the Liberals. After several attempts to get into Parliament he finally made it at a by-election in Birmingham in 1904, and faced Carson across the House. It was around this time that the two had the cream of their major court duels, though neither political nor any other difference ever spilled into personal animosity, they were both big enough men to keep them at the professional level.

Isaacs had come into the Archer-Shee case late in the day. He had only recently been appointed Solicitor General and up to the final stages most of the matter had been handled by lower level lawyers. When he studied the papers he found that in the pleadings two basic answers had been filed to the petition. One was a legal point that Mr Archer-Shee had no right to bring any petition in this matter, and the other an argument of fact, that George had stolen the postal order.

He then had a difficult decision to make: in what order should the points be taken? The legal point seemed a very strong one and if it were dealt with first then the case would probably collapse without any of the facts being heard and George would have no opportunity to vindicate himself. Isaacs's son in a biography* records that his father indulged in much heart searching and long and anxious reflection over his decision. Personally Sir Rufus Isaacs was inclined to waive the legal objection, but eventually he concluded that his duty as a Law Officer was to press it at the earliest opportunity, because if he did not

* Published by Hutchinson, 1942.

he would establish a dangerous precedent which might not be in the public interest. It might lead to any servant of the Crown who had been dismissed being able to sue successfully in the courts, something which had long been accepted as impossible and against the public interest.

The decision caused much argument later and Isaacs was widely criticised. Not all the critics were prepared to appreciate his position and responsibility, and it looked to many as if he were trying to aid the Admiralty to cover up a blunder. Where he seems to have erred is in not giving sufficient account to the special position of a naval cadet, for whom this was the only recourse to a tribunal of justice; almost any other category of Crown servant would have been given an opportunity to present his own defence properly. Writing some twenty years later Sir Derek Walker-Smith* concluded that in these circumstances it would have been better to allow a hearing on the facts first, and on a practical level events were to show this would have been the wisest course.

However Isaacs had decided differently. So as soon as the court met he was on his feet:

> My Lord, before the jury are sworn there is a point which arises on the pleadings with regard to the petition of right which is of very great importance, upon which I want to ask your Lordship's judgment, because it is a matter which goes to the very root of the case which is now before your Lordship. It involves this point that I say on behalf of the Crown, that a petition of right does not lie.

Carson had not really expected this, he had hoped he would be allowed to present his facts. His immediate reaction was to submit to the judge that this was not the stage at which to take such a point as they had come to try the case before a jury, but the judge told him at once he did not think he had any right to this.

Carson then argued his point, which was that a petition of right does not differ in principle from any other case, and in any other civil action Isaacs would not have succeeded in the move he was making. Carson pointed out that the Crown could have "taken out a summons" which would have led to the question he was raising being settled first, but now both sides had gone to considerable expense in preparing details of the facts and in getting their witnesses to court, and this should be heard.

* His excellent essay on legal aspects of the case appears in his *Lord Reading and his Cases*, Chapman & Hall, 1934.

Isaacs disagreed, a Petition of Right was different, he maintained. He was arguing a 'demurrer', a legal term even then virtually obsolete and retained only in a Petition of Right. Carson replied that Isaacs was merely playing semantics, and it would be absurd if all the expenses of preparing for a trial could be laid out, and then on arrival in court proceedings come to a grinding halt without any use being made of them. When the pleadings had been closed, he argued, the Crown could have asked for this demurrer to be dealt with first, and he added he had never heard of a similar thing happening before. The Judge sympathetically agreed that neither had he.

The two lawyers then embarked on a legal wrangle, with Carson pointing out that it was over a year since the petition had first been lodged and Isaacs returning that a Petition of Right was in a special category and that it was open to Carson, as soon as he had seen the demurrer on the pleadings, to ask the court to have it dealt with first.

Carson retorted that this suggestion, which the Judge supported, was unprecedented, and asked why they, who were challenging the action of the Government, should do so; had they not the right, he asked, to assume that the Admiralty would allow the facts to be tried?

The Judge intervened to say he was not sure about this, and so Carson emphasized his point by mentioning that the Admiralty had made arrangements through Lewis & Lewis to interview some of their witnesses, which had certainly given them the impression they expected the facts to be heard.

In the two decades preceeding this case there had been a number of procedural changes in the legislative system to modernise it, and older Judges sometimes had to tread warily to ensure that they were not still remembering the way things were done in their youth. At this point Mr Justice Ridley ordered a small adjournment while he consulted some references.

When he returned he announced that he took the preliminary view that the Crown were right and so Isaacs's demurrer could be considered first.

Despite this Carson then asked for the Jury to be sworn, as he wanted them to hear all that went on, a move which led to the first acrimonious exchange:

CARSON: Our desire is to have the issue of facts tried.
JUDGE: Yes, I quite understand the position.
CARSON: I do not understand the course my friend has taken.

ISAACS: That is an observation my friend is not entitled to make.

CARSON: I make it most deliberately.

ISAACS: You have no right to make that observation. The question
          whether or not we are right in the course we have taken is
          for My Lord to Judge.

CARSON: I have a perfect right to make that observation.

ISAACS: I dispute it.

CARSON: I say it is a scandal.

Isaacs wanted no more of this so he asked the Judge to continue
with swearing in the jury. There was a moment of light relief when
one juryman announced he was deaf and could not hear what was being
said. He was excused, and everyone agreed to continue with eleven
jurymen only.

Isaacs now had to argue his demurrer. The gist of it was that as a
cadet was a servant of the Crown the Petition of Right was not valid.
If he could establish this point he would undoubtedly be right, for it
was clearly established that a servant of the Crown could not sue for
wrongful dismissal. The main point on which he rested his case was a
sentence in the Osborne regulations:

All Naval Cadets enter the service under identical conditions and are
trained together until they pass for the rank of Lieutenant.

The crucial words being "enter the service".

He expounded the point in some detail, referring to the application
form Mr Archer-Shee had completed; he also explained the training
the cadets received, in which he got some help from Carson. He
concluded by coming back to his opening point:

That a Naval Cadet enters the service is the nub of the matter, and that is
the end.

Carson must have realised he now had a difficult task, for in strict
law Isaacs had a very strong case (his main contention was never
formally settled at any point in the proceedings but is almost certainly
sound). However Carson argued that this case bore no resemblance to a
claim by a servant of the Crown, it was a claim by a man who had a
contract with the Admiralty to educate his son for the Navy. In return
for this he had entered into certain obligations to make payments and to
ensure his son would subsequently enter the Navy.

Like Isaacs he also referred to the Osborne regulations, in particular to the two, Numbers 17 and 18, which dealt with the removal of a cadet. The first concerned those cadets who failed to reach a satisfactory standard, the second those whose conduct was unsatisfactory, and he said it was clear that the Admiralty had acted in George's case under the second. He maintained that under this regulation the Admiralty could make any allegation they liked without foundation, and dismiss a cadet with a permanent stigma attached. He also pointed out that if the Admiralty claimed that a cadet was subject to the Naval Discipline Act as all commissioned officers were then he could demand a court martial before being ruined for life.

He then attempted to compare the position with that of an ordinary schoolboy, and started on the lawyer's favourite game of quoting other cases. He mentioned *Fitzgerald v. Northcote** in which a father had brought an action against a schoolmaster for assault and false imprisonment of his son.

This led Mr Justice Ridley to a bit of irrelevance: "I recall I had an action before me once—a schoolmaster against a boy for setting his house on fire."

Carson seized the opportunity to make a point: "I suppose an opportunity was given of trying whether he did set it on fire?"

"Yes," replied the Judge, "we tried it out."

"Everywhere outside the Navy that would be so."

But the Judge was not to be drawn any further, he merely recalled: "I believe that it was found that he did it, if I remember aright."

Carson next turned to another case, *Hunt v. the Governors of Haileybury College.*† In this the Judge had made a number of observations about the power of schoolmasters over their charges and he had ruled that to give them arbitrary powers to brand a boy for life by expulsion was far too great and dangerous. When Carson had finished with some detailed legal points his chief assistant, Mr Leslie Scott, made an additional speech in support, with the main theme that this case was different from that of an ordinary naval officer because someone who was not an officer had agreed to pay for something to be done.

Isaacs replied to this by saying that it would be quite impossible for anyone to make the sort of contract which was being suggested on behalf of the Crown, as much a move would given an ordinary citizen an unprecedented position.

* 4 Foster & Finlason p. 656.
† *Times Law Reports*, Vol. 4 p. 623.

At this point the Judge interrupted to tell him he need not continue.

I am in favour of your point, Mr Solicitor, but as I suppose there will be an appeal and the appeal court might decide differently and the plaintiffs have come with the witnesses had we not better try the case?

Isaacs had made his legal point successfully, but Carson's arguments were receiving sympathy. Isaacs however refused to give way to this suggestion and told the Judge:

"I am entitled to your ruling."

This Mr Justice Ridley then gave. He said he was satisfied that a cadet was in the service of the Crown, and also that he could not recognise any distinction because a parent was sueing on behalf of a child.

The defeated Carson then raised the question of costs, and on these at least Isaacs was more amenable, agreeing that the Crown should only receive costs as if the demurrer had been heard, which meant that Mr Archer-Shee would not be billed for all their expenses in gathering evidence and bringing in witnesses: a small consolation.

It was while they were discussing these that Isaacs threw in an aside by which he laid himself open to Carson. He observed that "there have been various enquiries into the facts".

Carson retorted: "There has been no enquiry except one hole-in-the-corner enquiry in which a boy of 13 was never represented."

The Judge told him: "You are not entitled to say that," and Isaacs added: "I do not think you are entitled to say that when a King's Counsel went down. Mr George Elliot went down with Messrs. Lewis & Lewis to conduct the enquiry."

This rather misleading statement may be the reason why some writers have assumed that Mr Elliot was making an enquiry on behalf of the Admiralty. Carson came back: "There was an enquiry for the purpose of getting evidence which we are not allowed to read now before the court. It is a gross outrage."

"I do not think you ought to say that the court has been guilty of a gross outrage," admonished the Judge.

"Not the court," Carson assured him, "I say the Admiralty has been guilty of a gross outrage. Your Lordship has decided it the application by my friend."

Isaacs then gave him an even wider opening: "My friend has no right to say that without the facts being proved."

A.A.A.—G

"But," stormed a furious Carson, "you will not allow me to prove them!"

With great effect he then stalked out of court, leaving Mr Leslie Scott to tie up a few loose ends on the question of costs before everyone adjourned.

10
APPEAL

Mr Justice Ridley had been right when he assumed Carson would appeal. Just as soon as judgment had been delivered he presented himself in the higher court to make arrangements for them to hear his arguments. Instead of leaving most of the detailed work to his junior, Mr Hoffgaard, as would have been the normal practice, he took care of most of them personally, so strongly did he feel about the way things had developed. Isaacs and the Admiralty were equally anxious that no time should be wasted, in particular they did not want the naval witnesses hanging around away from their ships for any longer than was necessary, so they co-operated and so it was soon known that the appeal would be heard within a few days.

The press reports of the first hearing gave the public their first idea of what was in the wind. Only a few factual details had emerged but Carson's indignant display attracted attention. Most of the press confined itself to a factual account, but the *Morning Post* could not resist the opportunity. In its leader columns the writer observed that the court outburst by Carson would make most people anxious to get at the real facts of the case. He thought that the ordinary citizen would interpret the situation in one way only, that Mr McKenna and the Admiralty were fully determined that no full and impartial investigation of the case should take place. The suggestion was that this was because Mr McKenna knew himself to be in the wrong and so the Admiralty aim seemed to be to convert the constitutional maxim that "the King can do no wrong" into legal maxim that "Mr McKenna can do no wrong".

An idea of some current attitudes to Osborne came a few days later in a letter from a reader in the same paper. A Mr T. Addison Chater, presumably a schoolmaster, explained how he had been addressing a group of boys about the importance of the title Prince of Wales recently conferred on Prince Edward and had asked the group, forty-three in number, how many aspired to become naval officers, and the service was so popular that over a third, fifteen, had raised their hands. At about the same time a man "widely recognised as among the most efficient of our preparatory school headmasters" had told him that he believed that to encourage any young man to enter the Navy by way of Osborne College as at present constituted would, he felt, mean disloyalty to the life interests of such lads. Mr Chater concluded with an involved expression of patriotic anxiety.

The hopes of those who were anxious to know more now rested on a trio of Judges of the Court of Appeal, Lord Justices Vaughn Williams, Fletcher Moulton and Buckley. Everything was ready for Carson to present his arguments before them only six days after the first court appearance, the following Monday. They listened to several hours of legal argument from both sides with each of the distinguished legal trio on the bench intervening to discuss questions as they arose; they heard intricate points of law, regulations, and various authorities cited to try and help them decide if Mr Justice Ridley had been right.

Carson opened by explaining the position. He quickly made the point that under the Osborne arrangements Mr Archer-Shee could have been sued by the Admiralty if he had not made the payments he was required to make by the regulations, and he explained these regulations to the Judges in some detail. When the word 'demurrer' first came in they were a bit puzzled by it and queried if it was still in use, but Isaacs satisfied them that it was still a valid term in the exceptional case of a Petition of Right.

Carson endeavoured to claim that the situation at Osborne was akin to that at a public school, and that cadets were not yet in the Navy; he drew attention to the origin of the word cadet which seems to have come from France where it was applied to the son of a nobleman who was looking for an army commission.

He concentrated at some length on one previous case, *Grant v. The Secretary of State for India*, an involved matter concerning a former officer of the East India Company. When the Company had transferred all its duties and servants directly to the Crown there were some redundancies, and Grant, along with others, was asked to resign. This he refused to do and so he was forcibly placed on the retired list under various rules meant to deal only with incompetent officers or those who misbehaved, neither of which allegations applied to grant. He too had presented a petition of right, and though he had lost Carson felt that a number of the Judge's observations were in his favour.

Before he had finished his arguments Carson used some very strong language, talking about the Admiralty trumping up a charge which was totally devoid of any foundation.

Isaacs then had to reply to this, and to endeavour to demolish Carson's arguments. The Judges discussed a number of points with him and it soon began to emerge that they felt that as Mr Archer-Shee had been paying money there had been a contract. They asked Isaacs what would happen in the case of a cadet who was sent away from Osborne because the Admiralty alleged his father had not paid the fees due, and it was then found there had been a blunder and the money had been paid all along. Isaacs evaded this one by replying that in such circumstances the boy would, of course, be readmitted, but that it was most unlikely as fees had to be paid in advance anyway.

Lord Justice Vaughn Williams then raised another theoretical possibility with a strong topical association, that of a shipbuilder with a contract to build a Dreadnought. Isaacs replied that that was "very tender ground at present" and Vaughn Williams explained that what he had in mind was any contractor in such circumstances who was dismissed half way through the work, when, he felt, a petition of right would lie.

The feeling that the three Lords of Appeal were not very sympathetic to Isaacs was becoming more and more apparent. Eventually Lord Justice Vaughn Williams put the matter directly by saying:

"Yes, yes, but where are the facts? We want the facts." At this Isaacs felt it prudent to enquire: "I do not know if I understand your Lordships rightly. Is the indication of your Lordships' opinion that it would be better that the facts should be tried before the point of law is decided?" Lord Justice Vaughn Williams told him this was indeed their feeling, and Isaacs said he was prepared to accept this. He was probably not obliged to go along with the three Judges and could, as he had in the court below, have insisted on a judgment on his point of law. If he had it would probably have been decided in his favour, but he had some personal sympathy, whatever the Admiralty might think, with George's anomalous position, and so was probably quite happy to give way.

There was then a little more argument about procedure and agreement that the hearing should take place as soon as possible. Carson enquired about costs, and at first the Judges wanted to pass this to the Judge who presided over the final trial, but Carson, sensing that he was now facing some who were sympathetic to him, pressed the issue. He was rewarded by a two to one judgment in his favour, that the Crown would have to pay all costs of the previous hearing and this appeal.

Carson's skill and tenacity had been well rewarded, and at last all the facts were to be brought out in open court. The 'Long Vacation', or the Courts' summer holiday, was due shortly and so if there was not to be undue delay it was important once again to move fast. The Admiralty were equally anxious to get on with the matter and the public knew that a story of considerable interest could emerge. The Admiralty's many critics were watching and waiting.

11

THE FACTS AT LAST

With all-round co-operation everyone was ready for the next hearing after only a further eight days, on Tuesday 26th July. Now the gathering in the High Court was sure that at last they would learn all about the events at Osborne almost two years before. Enough had already emerged to whet the public appetite and the Court was therefore crowded from the beginning; the English summer had turned into an unusually overpowering heatwave and the atmosphere in the court room soon became hot and heavy.

The Judge trying the case was Mr Justice Philimore, not perhaps the happiest of choices. He came from a venerable legal family and had made his own name first as a barrister in two separate fields, the Admiralty Court (which dealt with shipping questions and had no connection with the sort of matter now being heard) and the Ecclesiastical Courts where he had become an authority on the sort of church matters which some Anglican Christians find so important, what vestments it is proper for a priest to wear and whether lighted candles should grace a communion table.

In the *Dictionary of National Biography* Lord Sankey writes that his appointment as a Judge in 1895 had come as something of a surprise and his limited experience had not fully equipped him for the whole range of work a Judge has to undertake. While in some fields he was undoubtedly able Lord Sankey admits, "On the Civil side of his work he was not always happy in the trial of an ordinary *nisi prius* case before a jury, and was wont to interrupt cross-examination of counsel". His handling of this case has seemed to some that he was very unsympathetic towards Carson and his client, but if viewed against his known background it is hard to see that this was really the case, despite some clashes with Carson.

The main aim of proceedings was to establish if George was the thief. As it was a civil case it would not follow the normal order of an English criminal trial when the prosecution states the case and the accused then attempts to refute it, but would be in reverse; in addition the court would also have to consider some associated matters as well as the theft itself. Carson would have to try and show not only that George was innocent, but also that the Osborne authorities and the Admiralty had acted hastily and not made proper investigations. If the Admiralty could convince the jury that they had acted 'in good faith' even though they may have made a mistake, then the chances of Mr Archer-Shee, who was the formal petitioner, getting any substantial damages were greatly reduced.

So Carson opened the proceeding, and began by explaining in detail what the case was all about. He did this with the most persuasive stops in his power of Irish advocacy pulled out, endeavouring to paint a picture of an upright and innocent young boy wronged by arrogant authority. He soon mentioned the handwriting report and Mr Gurrin and this led to his first clash with Mr Justice Philimore:

CARSON: I suppose Mr Gurrin will be produced when I shall have some more questions to ask him as to his previous experience.

JUDGE: I think that is an unworthy observation, Sir Edward.

CARSON: Why, My Lord?

JUDGE: I do not think it necessary. You know Mr Gurrin quite well, and you have very often called him a Counsel for the Crown.

CARSON: I do not remember ever calling him, My Lord.

JUDGE: I should be surprised if you had not done so.

CARSON: I resent your Lordship saying that it is an unworthy observation. Why should I not say that I have a question to ask him?

JUDGE: Everybody knows Mr Gurrin.

CARSON: I hope your Lordship will withdraw that observation.

JUDGE: I cannot, Sir Edward.

CARSON: Then I do not mind . . . I shall try not to be upset in this case.

Clearly Mr Justice Philimore was one of those easily hypnotised by the status of the 'expert', but Carson went on, making no further reference to his unnecessary interruption. He started to explain the events surrounding George's departure from Osborne and he read out the letter which had been sent to Mr Archer-Shee. He continued:

His son was branded as a thief and as a forger, a boy of 13 years old was labelled and ticketed, and has been since labelled and ticketed for all his future life as a thief and a forger, and in such investigation as had occurred which led to that disastrous result, neither his father nor any friend was ever there to hear what was alleged or what was said against a boy of 13 years of age, who by that one letter, and by that one determination was absolutely deprived of the possibility of any future career either in His Majesty's Service, or indeed in any other Service.

Gentlemen, I protest against the injustice to a little boy, a child of 13 years of age, without communication with his father or his parents, without his case ever being put, or an opportunity of its ever being put forward by those on his behalf—I protest against that boy at that early stage, a boy of that character, being branded for the rest of his life by that one act, an irretrievable act that I venture to think could never be got over. That little boy from that day, and from the day that he was first charged, up to this moment, whether it was in the ordeal of being called in before his Commander and his Captain, or whether it was under the softer influences of the persuasion of his own loving parents, has never faltered in the statement that he is an innocent boy.

Then he emphasized the long period which had elapsed since the events, during which they had pressed for an independent enquiry but it was not till they brought this petition of right that now it was possible, and even this was only after last-minute objections by the Crown had been overruled on appeal. He went on:

In that way we will now have the satisfaction of knowing that if this boy is to spend the rest of his life under this stigma as a thief and a forger it will not be by any inquiry of a department or any autocratic action of the State, but it will be by the verdict of 12 of his own citizens after they have thoroughly sifted the evidence, and be he right or be he wrong that, and that alone can be a satisfactory conclusion of this case. His father unhesitatingly puts him before you to try a charge of theft against him. He asks nothing but what the ordinary street arab would have for his own child—nay, not so much, because before the ordinary child of the street could be condemned and convicted he would at least have the protection of a grand jury, presided over by a Judge, and he would have the protection of a common jury afterwards presided over by a Judge, and the ultimate protection of the Court of Appeal.

He then told the Jury that as far as he and his client were concerned George was there to be tried on the plain issue whether he was a thief and forger or not, the Crown could make what they like of legal points afterwards. He continued with his detailing of events, emphasising the various Admiralty delays which had occurred when Lewis & Lewis first raised the matter. He made no mention of the communications or conference between Sir George Lewis and Lord Desart, as this had been agreed at the time; however this led the Admiralty to feel that this was unfairly exaggerating the delay, though they themselves had laid down the terms of the original meeting. It appeared that there had been a gap of over two weeks between the first letter and any response.

In his account of the enquiries at Osborne he dealt at some critical length on the part played by Lieutenant Burrows. He explained that it was a term officer's duty to look after the interests of his charges and claimed that the Lieutenant had not stood up for George in any way. He read out a long pre-trial interrogation of the Lieutenant in which he had been questioned about what he had done to help George, which had culminated in the answer: "I seem to have done very little."

Carson observed that in consequence the young boy had faced his accusers unaided, and commented, "I suggest to you that one of the most lamentable things in this case is that he did discharge the duty in the way in which he did discharge it."

Having thoroughly briefed judge and jury on all the details he then put Mr Archer-Shee into the witness box as his first witness. To give himself a rest he left the examination to his chief aide Mr Leslie Scott. Mr Scott was an able KC and fellow Conservative Member of Parliament, who is as well remembered for anything in that his Liverpool Chambers where he carved out his main career were the training ground for the brilliant young legal and political firework, Mr F. E. Smith.

He took Mr Archer-Shee through the details of what had happened and concentrated in particular on the abortive interview with Captain Christian at Osborne when he had gone to collect George, and on the delay before the Captain had even agreed to see him. He also asked how well the father knew his son's handwriting and if it compared with the signature on the stolen postal order; Mr Archer-Shee said that of course he knew his son's hand well and that it was not at all like that on the postal order; he felt quite well qualified to say this as he had some experience in handwriting matters in his bank work. This led the Judge to enquire if he had passed through the lower ranks of the bank and had ever served as a cashier at the counter, for he felt that cashiers could be almost experts in these matters; Mr Archer-Shee had however not done this.

Mr Archer-Shee then stood down, and his son followed him. The crowded public and press galleries now at last saw the centrepiece of the case, the fresh-looking young man whose character and honour so many people were prepared to make such efforts to vindicate. Unquestionably he would be a key witness and both the answers he gave and the general impression he made would be vital. First Carson took him gently through the events of the afternoon of the theft and the various enquiries, and finally obtained from the boy an emphatic reaffirmation that he had nothing to do with the theft or the cashing of the postal order.

Carson then sat and Isaacs stood. This was to be the most testing time and Carson and the Archer-Shee family watching knew that the next few hours would be decisive. The boy faced as dangerous a cross-examiner as he was likely to meet, and though doubtless as much as possible had been done to prepare him now he was alone in the wooden-sided enclave with a chance to prove himself to judge, jury and the world, or to leave disgraced for ever.

Isaacs's line soon became clear: he was going to worry over details of the afternoon of the theft to see if he could trap George in any way, and in particular he would concentrate on those parts of his account where he was vague in details of his movements or they seemed difficult to understand.

He opened by trying to find out if George had known that Back had received the postal order that morning and got the answer that he had known nothing about it until after the loss. He then briefly raised a point he was later to hammer heavily.

ISAACS: Is there a rule that you must not go into the reading room between two and three o'clock!

GEORGE: Yes.

ISAACS: During that hour, I suppose, at any rate, if it is fine you have to be out?

GEORGE: Yes.

ISAACS: So that if you went into the reading room between two and three on that day you were going in disobedience of orders?

GEORGE: Yes.

ISAACS: Was there also a rule that you should not keep money in the reading room, or any articles of value in your locker?

GEORGE: Yes, I think there was.

ISAACS: If you put money away you were supposed to put it away in your till, were you not?

GEORGE: Yes, or carry it about with you.

Then he moved on through George's movements and also asked about the clothes he had been wearing at the time and the number of pockets in which he could put money; but shortly he returned to his key point about what he had done immediately after he had collected his money from the College Bank just after Medical Inspection.

ISAACS: When you got the money you walked with it and put it in your locker in the reading room?

GEORGE: Yes.

ISAACS: While you changed. Then after you had changed you went back into the reading room?

GEORGE: I went to watch the roller skating.

ISAACS: And then you went into the reading room?

GEORGE: Yes.

ISAACS: Did you never have any money in your pocket?

GEORGE: We have no trousers pocket.

ISAACS: You have a coat pocket?

GEORGE: Yes, but only in here, and I was not accustomed to putting money in those pockets.

ISAACS: Had you a pocket in your trousers which you had worn before you had changed into flannels?

GEORGE: No, except just a very small flap pocket.

ISAACS: You were going straight up to change?

GEORGE: Yes.

ISAACS: If that was the case, why did you not take the money with you and go straight into the dormitory to change? Why would you have put it in the reading room at all?

GEORGE: There is nowhere to put it in your chest while you are changing.

ISAACS: Think! You go into your room to change your things, and you would have to go back to the reading room, which would be against orders, to get the money. The simple way would appear to be for you to take the money in your hand straight to the dormitory where you are going to change, and bring the money away with you. That would appear to be the simpler course, would it not?

GEORGE: It is only a matter of a yard or two, and coming out of the dormitory you are allowed to go into the reading room to get anything before you go out. What they mean is staying in the reading room before three.

ISAACS: You mean you can go in if you like to fetch anything, but you must not stay, supposing you come out of the dormitory. It still remains that you did not do that?

GEORGE: No, I did not. I went to watch the roller skating first.

ISAACS: I want to see what you say with reference to it. When you did come back to go into the reading room would be acting against orders?

GEORGE: Yes, unless I had leave.

ISAACS: Unless you had leave to go into the reading room to fetch it?

GEORGE: Yes.

ISAACS: Did you ask anybody for leave?

GEORGE: No, not that I remember.

ISAACS: Do you not know quite well that you never did ask anybody's leave to go into the reading room?

GEORGE: I am not sure, but I believe I asked the Chief Petty Officer if I could go to the post office before I went into the reading room for my money.

ISAACS: That does not answer the question I am putting to you. You told us before it was after, and I will ask you about that in a minute. Leave out about asking the Chief Petty Officer whether you could go to the post office. What I am asking you is, do you not know quite well that you never asked anybody's leave to go into the reading room to fetch your money?

GEORGE: No, not that I remember.

ISAACS: I will put it to you again. If that was the case, according to your story, you had got the money from the officer, a sixteen-shilling chit, and you were going from there straight to change?

GEORGE: Yes.

ISAACS: You were then going to get into your flannels and coming down intending to go to the post office after you had got leave, I suppose?

GEORGE: Yes.

ISAACS: I must ask you again why, under those circumstances, you did not go with your money straight up to your room to

change, and why you say you went into the reading room
and put the money into the locker?

GEORGE: I did not want the money hanging about me until I did
actually want to go to the post office.

All in all George was standing up very well, and had not made a
single slip. Soon afterwards he gave as good as he got as Isaacs continued by worrying him about what he normally did when he had
money at the College:

ISAACS: I suppose you sometimes took money out of your pocket to
pay for things at the canteen?

GEORGE: When you buy things you usually pay for them.

It was now getting near the end of the day and Isaacs still had a long
way to go; the only other important point he concentrated on that
afternoon was the allegation that George had admitted practising
Back's signature, and that he had offered this as his explanation when
the Commander had commented on his knowing Back's Christian
name. George firmly denied that he had either practised Back's signature or claimed to have done so.

The Judge then adjourned until the next morning. At half past ten
on Wednesday they all reassembled a little fresher and less tired,
though the oppressive heat of the court was causing some bother.
Isaacs immediately returned to his main line of attack.

ISAACS: You could have put money into your trouser pocket or into
one of your coat pockets?

GEORGE: Yes.

ISAACS: And if you had done that and had gone to the dormitory to
change, the money would be in the coat pocket all the time,
when you went into the dormitory and when you came out
again to go to the post office?

GEORGE: Yes.

ISAACS: And there would be no necessity for you to put it into the
locker in the reading room, or to take it out?

GEORGE: I do not know why I did put it there.

ISAACS: It is the reason that is puzzling, and that is what I wanted
to ask you for. You cannot give any explanation of why you
did it?

GEORGE: I just put it there while I went to change. I thought it would be quite safe there, and I did not want it knocking about in the dormitory.

ISAACS: Why should it be knocking about in the dormitory when you were going to the dormitory to get your things changed? You would be in the dormitory the whole time while you changed and the money would be with you. How would it be knocking about in the dormitory?

GEORGE: Because I usually take off my coat.

ISAACS: But suppose you did, you would be there and it would be put by the side of you?

GEORGE: Yes, I know.

ISAACS: There would be no danger in that?

GEORGE: I cannot remember any special reason why I did put it in the reading room.

ISAACS: It was a very unusual thing to do?

GEORGE: I do not think so.

ISAACS: Was it not a very unusual thing to put money into your locker?

GEORGE: I do not think it very unusual.

ISAACS: Was it not unusual to put loose money, not a postal order or anything of that kind, but loose money, into the locker?

GEORGE: It was not unusual amongst the cadets.

ISAACS: It occurs to you now as a rather curious proceeding, in view of this, that you were going to change, and would have the money with you all the time?

GEORGE: I do not see that it is particularly peculiar.

ISAACS: You cannot give us any information, other than you have done, as to why you did that?

GEORGE: I cannot give any explanation.

After asking a little more about the various investigations, and also clarifying some details of the geography of Osborne, Isaacs came to what was probably his most dangerous point, the time question. He asked George if, when first interviewed by Captain Christian, he had claimed to have gone to the post office between three and four o'clock; he received a disarmingly frank reply:

"As far as I remember I think I did, but I corrected myself afterwards if I remember rightly."

"At the same interview or later?" enquired the Judge.

"I fancy at the same interview."

Isaacs pressed the point further, suggesting to George that he had not actually made the correction until some time afterwards "when Lewis & Lewis had come on the scene". George's memory was a bit uncertain, though he denied this and finished off with a resolute declaration:

"All I can say is if I said to Captain Christian that it was between three and four o'clock I made a mistake."

With that Isaacs had fired his last shot, and after asking about the break-in into George's own till a few days after the theft he sat down. It was clear he had not inflicted too much damage and when Carson rose for a brief re-examination he knew his faith in the boy was fully justified.

He had only a few minor points to clear up, the main one being about the signature on the stolen postal order. He was soon in a discussion with the Judge and Isaacs about whether it was alleged this was an attempt to forge Back's genuine signature or to copy the name as written at the top of the postal order. Carson said he thought Isaacs was implying the former but was assured that this was not so.

Carson then brought in once more the question of George going into the reading room during the forbidden hour between two and three o'clock. From the witness box George explained that the reading room was very near where they had been watching roller skating, just inside a covered way, and it was not unusual for a cadet to go quickly to fetch something; it was long stays at the time when they were supposed to be getting fresh air and exercise which caused complaint.

Finally the Judge decided to clarify a few points, and any hostility he may have had to the case Carson was presenting is not shown in the few gentle questions he put to George. He enquired what a cadet was supposed to do with any money he received during the term and George told him he thought they were supposed to put it in the college bank; he also asked George if, by any chance, he was in debt at all and the boy assured him he was not.

That was all, and George was allowed to step down, having at least created a favourable impression and having made no slip of any sort.

Carson next called the witness who could most readily support some of George's story, Patrick Scholes. Scholes was able to confirm that his friend had asked him to join him on a walk to the post office at the time of around half past two, which he knew was right because his friends

(*right*) Major Martin Archer-Shee DSO MP

(*left*) George Archer-Shee – a picture that originally appeared in *The Illustrated London News* in 1910

(*left*) Sir Edward Carson KC MP

(*below*) A scene in court: Terence Back in the witness box

had arrived shortly afterwards, and he also recalled him going into the reading room and coming out again "after two or three minutes".

In cross-examination Isaacs asked him if when George had first approached him he had said he was going to the post office to "get" or to "cash" a postal order, a difference of some significance. Scholes replied that he said "get", though a little confusion was promptly caused by the Judge not hearing aright the first time. This was sorted out and Scholes repeated "get" emphatically.

This questioning now proved to be a mistake for Isaacs, for it was the first Carson had heard about this and so he had a shrewd idea what had been going on on the Crown side. It was now his turn to re-examine and he immediately asked Scholes when it had first been suggested to him that George might have said "cash"; Scholes replied that this was when the Treasury Solicitor enquired about it the previous day. Isaacs immediately intervened to explain that this had been done at his request merely to settle a doubt in his own mind.

"I do not suggest anything improper on the part of the Treasury Solicitor," responded Carson dryly, but a glance towards the jury told him that they did not like this last-minute suggestive questioning of the young witness.

Scholes was followed by George Arbuthnot who described his own visit to the post office, which he said was the first time he had been there in six terms at Osborne. He recalled seeing a cadet servant going in as he left but had no idea who he was. Isaacs asked him about the various paths between the college and the post office and it came out that there were three different routes of which George had used to and Arbuthnot the third, eliminating the possibility they might have met each other.

The telegraph boy, Frederick Langley, next told the court in answer to an examination by Mr Scott that he clearly recalled that only two cadets had come into the post office that afternoon, and that the second one had arrived soon after the first one left and he must have been gone by half past two. Cross-examining Isaacs tried to show his memory could easily be at fault as he had only had cause to think about the events when he was first questioned "some weeks later". It came out that Langley was now out of work, which caused the Judge to comment, "The post office is really to blame—like many other people they employ boys until they are too old for anything."

Isaacs then subjected Langley to a rapid-fire series of questions to test his memory on details and succeeded in showing there were many gaps. However Mr Scott in re-examination was able to nullify some of the effect of this because he got Langley to tell him he had been in the post office when the first telephone call came through from college and so the matter had been in his mind from the beginning. More help came from the Judge, who asked if he could recall which of the two cadets had stayed in the post office longest, and Langley replied the first, which tallied with the other statements that Arbuthnot had been kept waiting while Mr De Smit sent his telegrams.

Carson had now called all his witnesses on the basic facts, but he finished his case by adding several who attested to George's character. First was Major Martin, of whom he started with the cynical enquiry:

"Now you have the misfortune, I think, of being a Member of Parliament?"

"I have."

Then the Major described how straightforward a boy he found his young half-brother, and he was also asked for his views on the handwriting. He said that the only letter in the forged signature he thought at all like George's handwriting, which he knew well, was the 'k' with a little tick, but he added that all boys of that age tended to write similarly.

Isaacs used his opportunity to cross-examine to draw out details of the various enquiries which had taken place, to try and show that the Admiralty had not been as hasty and high-handed as Carson was implying.

Finally Carson called five people who knew George well, Father Henry Davis, and Mr Gordon Gorman of Stonyhurst, Mr Francis Streetell who had been Mr Archer-Shee's immediate deputy at the Bank in Bristol and knew all the family, Mr Livesey his Osborne tutor, and to end with the Principal of Stonyhurst, Father Bodkin. All used such adjectives as "straightforward", "truthful" and "honest" to describe George. This emphasis on character would not have been of great importance if the facts had been overwhelmingly against George for the jury would have known that someone of the best character can succumb to a momentary temptation. They served however to emphasize, if they accepted his innocence, how wrongfully the Admiralty had behaved; they also gave Isaacs a wide opening to call anyone else who might hold an opposite view, if he had been able to find any. At this point Carson closed his case.

And it was now Isaacs's turn.

12
ISAACS'S TURN

The court was becoming increasingly hot and crowded when Isaacs opened the case for the Crown. Now that proceedings were well into their second day, and the first day had been fully reported in the morning papers public interest was growing, and people had found their way into every corner of the courtroom, and were even cluttering up the passages leading in. The heat was particularly trying to Carson who was having one of his frequent bouts of feeling unwell.

Isaacs started with a formal reference to his demurrer, submitting that there was no case to answer, but adding that this would be dealt with later. He then launched into a lengthy speech which he started by recalling how Carson had emphasised the importance of the matter to George; but he pointed out that as an attack had been launched on the Admiralty it was therefore just as important to them.

He told the jury that his main evidence would come when he put Miss Tucker in the witness box, and they would also hear how steps that had been taken to get her statement at the earliest possible moment while events were still fresh in her mind. He explained that there would be a conflict between his evidence and that given earlier about the time George had gone to the post office; he also defended the use of Mr Gurrin to give an opinion on the handwriting as "the only course available", and promised that the expert would also appear in court.

He summed up his task:

"I have to justify the course the Admiralty has taken . . . an important point that strikes vitally at the honour and integrity of the administration—they honestly came to the conclusion and were bound to act as they did."

Miss Tucker now came to the witness box, an elderly lady, slightly short-sighted, who must have found the proceedings as much of an ordeal as anyone in court, including George. As Isaacs needed a rest from the long speech he had just made, the lady was cross-examined by his deputy, Mr Avory, an experienced criminal advocate soon to be promoted to the bench where he made a considerable mark as a fair and just judge.

He first took Miss Tucker through some of her duties at the Osborne Post Office; she explained that her hours of duty on the day had been in three shifts, from seven to nine in the morning, from half past one until five in the afternoon, and finally from six to eight-fifteen in the evening; she said she would have been alone behind the counter during these periods. Avory took her through the details of the afternoon of the theft and Miss Tucker handed the court the book in which she had recorded details of all postal order transactions during that period.

She then emphatically recalled that on that afternoon only two cadets had come into the office. She remembered how the first (Arbuthnot) had had some difficulty over the way he signed a postal order he wanted to cash; it was made payable to "George Arbuthnot" but when he first handed it in he had signed it only with an initial, G. Arbuthnot, and he had to alter this to match what was on the payee line. She also explained how Arbuthnot's stay had been prolonged by Mr De Smit's arrival with his telegrams.

Now she came to the contested parts of her evidence, and first insisted that the second cadet (George) had not arrived in the office until around an hour after the first. Avory asked her what business this cadet had done:

MISS TUCKER: He gave me a five-shilling postal order to cash.

AVORY: That was the first thing he did?

MISS TUCKER: Yes.

AVORY: He gave you a five-shilling postal order to cash. Did you notice anything about the order before you cashed it?

MISS TUCKER: Yes. I took it to the other side of the counter to get the cash and I saw 'Royal Naval College' on it. I took the money in my hand, and the postal order as well, and I said to the cadet: "This should not have been erased". It was crossed through.

AVORY: Did he say anything?

MISS TUCKER: Yes. He said: "It was like that when I got it."

AVORY: Did you then cash it?

MISS TUCKER: Yes.

AVORY: What did you give him in change for it?

MISS TUCKER: I gave him two half-crowns.

AVORY: What next happened? Did he do any more business?

MISS TUCKER: No, not just then. I took the postal order across the room to the stamping board and stamped it. I then went from the stamping board to the counter and initialled the postal order, and as I was putting it into the drawer I was asked for a fifteen-and-six postal order and a one-penny stamp.

AVORY: As you put the postal order that you had cashed into the drawer at the counter you were still facing the cadet at the counter?

MISS TUCKER: Yes, I was facing the counter. The cadet was on the other side of the counter. He was at one end and I was at the other.

AVORY: What did you say he asked you for?

MISS TUCKER: A postal order for fifteen-and-six and a one-penny stamp.

AVORY: Did he give you the money for that?

MISS TUCKER: Yes, he gave me half a sovereign and six shillings in three florins.

AVORY: You then issued him a postal order for fifteen-and-six?

MISS TUCKER: Yes.

AVORY: What change did you give him?

MISS TUCKER: I gave him threepence-halfpenny.

AVORY: That would be the right change, would it?

MISS TUCKER: Yes.

AVORY: Was anything said when you put the threepence-halfpenny down?

MISS TUCKER: He said something but I was not quite sure what it was, and I went to see if he had given me one of the half-crowns. I thought possible that he might have given me one of the half-crowns I had given him instead of what I supposed was a two-shilling piece. It was on the counter and I found that the three florins were there. I went back to him and said "It is quite right, the threepence-halfpenny change. The postal order is a penny-halfpenny."

After an intervention by the Judge to ensure that this point was absolutely clear Avory asked his key question:

"Was it the same cadet who cashed the five-shilling postal order?"

Before Miss Tucker could answer Carson stood and objected to "the question put in that term". The Judge would not accept this, he thought it quite proper, and Carson had to be content with being told that his objection would be "recorded somewhere". Miss Tucker them emphatically reaffirmed that the two postal orders had been handled by the same cadet. Avory ended his examination by taking her through the various occasions on which she had been questioned both at the college and at the post office in London.

Now it was the time for Carson's key cross-examination; the main cause of their complaint at not being allowed to be present at the earlier enquiries was that they had not been able to put this key witness to proper test. The whole cause would depend on what followed now, and if Carson could break Miss Tucker's story, or at least throw sufficient doubt on it to convince the jury that she might well be in error then he would win; if not then the fight to vindicate George would come to an inglorious end. Many and advocate might have tried to bully and frighten the lady to defeat, but this was not Carson's way. Had he done so he could easily have lost the jury's sympathy, but he used his immense skill to dominate her unnoticeably and approached her with a manner of gentle courtesy.

The identification question was his first point, and the lady readily agreed that she had not been able to identify any of the cadets, and also that she had said she thought the voice of the boy who had cashed the postal order had been "gruffer and thicker" than George's. Next Carson turned to the statement which Miss Tucker had signed after being interviewed by Captain Christian. She explained how it had been brought down to her at the post office, and retyped after she had objected to being called "Postmistress", and that all she had then done was to add her signature. Carson enquired if the pencil annotation "But she could not identify him" had been there at this point and she said she was sure it was not; the Judge suggested it had probably been put on afterwards.

Carson followed this with enquiries about the contents of the statement, and he asked Miss Tucker if the order of events given in it (that the cadet who had bought the fifteen-and-six postal order had been the same one who had cashed the five-shilling one) was in the right order. She admitted that it was the wrong way round.

Carson's main aim throughout his questioning was to emphasize two related points, firstly that Miss Tucker could be mistaken on her key facts, and secondly that this error could have arisen through some suggestive questioning at the beginning of the enquiries at Osborne. He dealt first with CPO Paul's visit to the post office:

CARSON: Did he ask you if a cadet came in and cashed a five-shilling postal order?
MISS TUCKER: Yes, he did ask me.
CARSON: Did he suggest that a cadet did?
MISS TUCKER: I do not think there was a suggestion in it.
JUDGE: Did he use the word 'cadet'? Instead of saying "Did a man come in?" did he say "Did a cadet come in?" which would show that he thought he was a cadet. Did he use the phrase 'cadet'?
MISS TUCKER: I believe so.
CARSON: Did Petty Officer Paul say that a boy had signed an order which had been cashed, and that he was not the boy to whom it was payable?
MISS TUCKER: No, I do not think so; I do not remember it. He may have done so, but I do not remember it at all.
CARSON: Will you deny that he said that?
MISS TUCKER: I do not remember it; I will not deny it.

She continued on this line of vague uncertainty until Carson moved on to something else CPO Paul had said to her:

CARSON: Did he say such people were not wanted in the Navy?
MISS TUCKER: Yes, he did.
CARSON: Have you ever seen Paul since to talk to?
MISS TUCKER: No.
CARSON: Was Paul in a very excited condition?
MISS TUCKER: He seemed to be rather annoyed.
CARSON: Was he excited?
MISS TUCKER: I thought he was; but I had never seen him before, so of course I could not say what his usual manner was.
CARSON: It might have been his natural manner?
MISS TUCKER: It might have been.

CARSON: Did it occur to you that he was excited?

MISS TUCKER: Yes, I thought so.

CARSON: Was he almost raving?

MISS TUCKER: I am afraid I said so, but I fancy that is rather exaggerated.

CARSON: But you would not say anything exaggerated in an important case of this kind, would you?

MISS TUCKER: I may have done in that case.

What Carson was trying to discover was exactly when the idea that a cadet was the thief had first been made to Miss Tucker. The Judge had been intervening quite often around this time.

CARSON: Did you ever tell anybody it was the cadet who cashed the order until you saw Commander Cotton?

JUDGE: Did you ever tell Paul or anybody that it was the cadet who cashed the order until you saw Commander Cotton?

MISS TUCKER: I believe so. I believe I did, but I am not quite sure.

CARSON: Here is what you said: "When I saw the Commander he and I and Mr Gordon were alone together. This was about ten-thirty. I saw the Commander in Mr Gordon's office. I had never been to the college before. I don't think Mr Gordon stayed all the time with Commander Cotton at my interview. By the time I got to Commander Cotton I had a general idea that a postal order had been stolen, and I knew the inquiry concerned a cadet. Commander Cotton asked me about the order and I told him. It was then for the first time that I stated that it was a cadet who had cashed the order"?

MISS TUCKER: If that was my statement it must be correct.

CARSON: Therefore I think I may take it you never made an allegation against the cadet until you saw Commander Cotton.

Carson also spent some time testing the lady's memory on matters in general.

CARSON: Now can you tell me anybody else who went in and had a transaction that day?

MISS TUCKER: No, I do not remember.

CARSON:	Come. Cannot you recollect anyone else having a conversation?
MISS TUCKER:	No, I certainly cannot.
CARSON:	How many went in that day?
MISS TUCKER:	A good many people would have come in, but there may not have been anything—
CARSON:	There may, or may not, but was there? Can you recollect?
MISS TUCKER:	No.
CARSON:	Can you recollect the appearance of anyone else?
MISS TUCKER:	No.
CARSON:	Can you recollect whether any cadet servants were in there?
MISS TUCKER:	No, I cannot.
CARSON:	Can you recollect that after Arbuthnot went away a cadet servant came in?
MISS TUCKER:	No, I do not remember.
CARSON:	You see Arbuthnot says that as he was going out a cadet servant came in?
MISS TUCKER:	Yes.
CARSON:	That your attention was drawn to when Mr Elliott was there?
MISS TUCKER:	That was a very long time afterwards. There was nothing to make me remember that.
JUDGE:	Was that in January?
CARSON:	November. Then you cannot call to mind any other person from that day except the cadets?
MISS TUCKER:	No, I could not.
CARSON:	Nor what they did?
MISS TUCKER:	No.
CARSON:	Nor what they said?
MISS TUCKER:	No.
CARSON:	Nor any other day?
MISS TUCKER:	I did not see any cadet. I only saw two cadets as far as I know.

He closed with a few more questions on similar lines, and some to find out if anyone else had made any similar memory tests at the earlier enquiries, which they had not.

Even though Carson had not succeeded in breaking Miss Tucker's story his brilliant cross-examination, still cited as a model of its type, had succeeded in doing considerable damage to her credibility; the jury and all present in court were left with the impression of a very uncertain woman who could easily be in error, even though she herself was clearly convinced that she was not. His gentle and persuasive manner had shown her, without her being aware of it, to be an unsure witness who may well have had her story suggested to her subconsciously by the way she had been approached at the start, and he must have known as he sat down that unless Isaacs had a surprise up his sleeve all his efforts were not wasted.

It was now late in the afternoon and everyone in court felt hot, tired and muggy; the robes and wigs which judge and counsel wear in British courts are far from ideal for a semi-tropical atmosphere. Isaacs took the re-examination for the Crown himself, but there was not a great deal he could do to improve his position, and it was somewhat perfunctory.

He tried to draw attention to the undisputed incidents which had impressed themselves on Miss Tucker's memory, such as the wrong signature by Arbuthnot and the change-giving incident with George. When he asked her if she had made the same statement she made now when she had been questioned by Mr Acland Carson immediately objected, and after the Judge had had a wrangle with Isaacs, this objection was upheld. The re-exaimination ended with Isaacs trying to elicit more details about the first telephone call from the college, under the rules of evidence he was now free to explore this as Carson had opened the issue, but the lady could recall little. That was the end of the day, and the Judge adjourned.

The following morning Carson told the Judge at the opening that he was feeling far from well. The Judge sympathised and said he felt that part of the problem was the heat; he warned the public gallery that he would welcome any opportunity to clear them out and if they gave him a chance he would do so; there had been some muttered interruptions during the previous day.

The Crown's first witness of the day was Terence Back, who was examined by Avory. He told how he had received the postal order in the morning post at breakfast and had put it in his locker. During the afternoon he had gone 'pulling', and when he had returned he had found it gone; it was just after this that he met George at the reading room door. He was certain that this could not have happened before half past three which tended to support Miss Tucker's estimate of the time. He supported George's denial that they had ever practised each other's signatures and also said that the crossing out of the words "Royal Naval College" on his postal order had not been his work.

On cross-examination Carson discovered that Back and George had sat some way apart and at different tables at breakfast when the postal order had arrived and there was no evidence that George had seen the postal order at any time. Back admitted that he too had broken the rules by putting the postal order into his locker, but he claimed that it was a rule often ignored. He and George had sat at adjacent desks for their first term at Osborne and so would have seen each other sign their names. He remembered that when he had told CPO Paul about the theft the Chief had received the news with considerable excitement, but he could not recall who had brought the name Archer-Shee into the conversation first.

Paul came next and told Isaacs very precisely that he had served in the Royal Navy for twenty-four years and ten months; since the events at Osborne he had retired with a pension. He remembered being on duty near the flagstaff when George had asked for leave to go to the post office and though he was uncertain about the time he thought it must have been near three o'clock as it was some while after Arbuthnot's similar request.

He had first heard about the theft from another Cadet, Butt, and had immediately sent for Back. Soon afterwards he reported the matter to Gunner Gordon and telephoned the post office. In answer to a question about what he had said to Miss Tucker he gave a surprising reply, he had asked her which of "the two cadets" who had been to the post office that afternoon had cashed the postal order, and Miss Tucker had told him it was the second.

This was both a clear contradiction of Miss Tucker's statement and also evidence of the suggestive questioning which Carson had already tried to imply. As it was now time for the cross-examination Carson took up the point immediately:

CARSON: Are you quite certain that before you went down to the post office that evening the postmistress had told a cadet had cashed the postal order?

PAUL: Yes.

CARSON: You are quite certain of that?

PAUL: Yes.

CARSON: Then if the postmistress has sworn that the first time she

stated a cadet had cashed the order was to Commander
Cotton the next day, that would not be true?

PAUL: It would not be true.

CARSON: She is inaccurate?

PAUL: She informed me through the telephone.

CARSON: Never mind about that, the postmistress must be inaccurate
          if she says that?

PAUL: Yes.

It was very clear that two of Isaacs's key witnesses had contradicted
each other on an important point, and if the Chief Petty Officer was
right then it was also further indication that Miss Tucker's memory
could be faulty. Next Carson took Paul onto sensitive ground and his
first visit to the post office, when Miss Tucker had said he was so over-
excited that he was "almost raving"; not surprisingly the Chief denied
this.

Carson then turned to the break-in into George's own till on the
Friday after the theft and asked Paul if he had ever suggested that
George himself might have been responsible for this; Paul replied
that he had not, but unfortunately for him Carson had some notes
taken by Mr Spickernell, the college Paymaster, at one of the enquiries
in which he was recorded as saying just this. All of which further dam-
aged Isaacs's case.

Gunner Gordon came next and explained the enquiries which had
been made when the theft had first been reported. On cross-examination Carson asked about his general impression of George and he
replied that he regarded the boy "as quite the average cadet"; at the
enquiries his manner had been very self-possessed and had impressed
him favourably; however under further questioning from the Judge he
admitted that there had been something, "an indefinable something"
were his words, which worried him but which he could not explain.

Gunner Gordon had served for seven years at Osborne and knew
the place and its people as well as anyone, so on re-examination
Isaacs enquired about cadets' habits with money in general; Gordon
told him that losses through carelessness were not uncommon, and
also that he had no reason to suspect the honesty of any of the cadet
servants.

The next witness was the Judge Advocate, Mr Acland, and his
arrival in the box was the sign for Carson to prepare himself for a
forceful exchange with the Judge. Isaacs opened his examination by

getting from Mr Acland the details of his duties, trying to emphasise that he was an independent judicial officer, and not the total servant of the Admiralty that Carson had implied. However as soon as he moved on to the enquiry Carson objected, and told the Judge that the only part of these enquiries he considered admissible was the questioning of George when Mr Poole and Major Martin had been present; for the rest they had been unrepresented, and though they had asked for the right to be present this had been abruptly refused. The Judge was unsympathetic and Isaacs was allowed to continue though Carson carried on with repeated objections which culminated in a bitter exchange with the Judge:

CARSON: I should like to know how far this is going to be admitted against us. I submit these matters were done behind our back, and cannot be given in evidence.

JUDGE: Once and for all I must tell you that I do not intend to take the view that these things were done behind your back any more than I should in a case where a Judge held an enquiry without the presence of the parties. They were done just as much behind the back of the Crown as they were done behind your back.

CARSON: That is nothing to do with me; the Crown is not being tried.

JUDGE: If you use the expression "done behind your back" it implies favouring one side or the other. If you say that it was done in your absence that is another thing.

CARSON: If your Lordship pleases I put it in that way or in any way so long as I get my point raised.

Mr Acland then gave a brief and sketchy account of his enquiry, making no mention of the somewhat subjective factors which had led him to his conclusion. He brought out nothing new, so when it was Carson's turn to cross-examine he was able to achieve considerable effect with a handful of simple questions all directed to one point.

CARSON: You said you were recorder of Oxford?

ACLAND: I am.

CARSON: I suppose if you were to try a boy for theft as Recorder of Oxford you would give an opportunity to both sides of being heard?

ACLAND: I could not do otherwise.

CARSON: I think so. The Crown would be represented and probably
          the prisoner?
ACLAND: Yes.
CARSON: I suppose when you are at sessions the same thing happens?
ACLAND: Yes.
CARSON: That would be a trial?
ACLAND: That would be a trial.

Mr Acland then left the witness box and was replaced by Lieutenant
Burrows, about whom Carson had been so critical in his opening
speech. However he did not now embarrass the young officer by
taking him through this again; he did however tackle him on the
rules about cadets going into the reading room between two and three
o'clock and the Lieutenant agreed that a quick visit such as George
had admitted would be a very minor matter, and had he found him in
there he would probably have done no more than tell him to "hurry on
out".

Two cadet servants, Pritchard and Mason, then made brief appearances without adding much except that Pritchard agreed that he
had probably been to the post office that afternoon; he recalled that one
day about that time he had been there to buy a postal order for Cadet
Startin.

The next witness for the Crown was the man on whom most of the
early enquiries had centred, Commander Stapleton-Cotton. In
straightforward manner the Commander told about the first steps he
had taken after the theft had been reported to him, which had started
with a telegram to Back's aunt, Miss Robinson, to find if she had
recorded the number of the postal order she had sent her nephew.

He then described the various interviews he had, and was sure
that when he first saw George he thought the boy had told him he had
gone to the post office around three o'clock, though he could not be
certain of this. He was however certain that George had explained
the way he signed Back's name by saying that they had been practising
each other's signatures in the reading room a few days before. He
had then asked Back about this, and had received a categorical denial
that any such thing had taken place.

When he recalled his conversation with Chief Petty Officer Paul
he brought in something completely new; he said the Chief had told
him that he knew he had given George leave shortly after three o'clock
as he remembered it had been a few minutes after he had sounded six

bells on the college bell which he had had to do on this occasion, though it was not normally his duty, as the sentry who should have done it was away on an errand. There is no record that the Chief mentioned this to anyone on any other occasion, both in court and at the various enquiries he was always somewhat vague about the time.

The Commander was undoubtedly a good witness, giving his answers in a clear, no-nonsense way which could at least have gone some distance to mitigating the impression that the Osborne authorities had acted in a hasty, ill-considered way. He explained how he had carefully collected all the evidence together before taking the matter to Captain Christian. Then he had put everything down in a letter which he had taken to the Captain personally, with a verbal explanation as well.

As soon as the letter was mentioned Carson asked to see it. Isaacs at first objected to this on the principle that it was a privileged communication by a servant of the Crown, but this time the Judge sympathised with Carson and Isaacs did not press his point, and read out the letter. It contained only a brief recital of the facts the Commander had discovered, but however a slight doubt was cast on his claims to careful accuracy as he referred to the postal order George had brought as being for sixteen-and-sixpence throughout.

Isaacs then finished his examination by going more fully into the investigations at Osborne, and it was now getting towards the end of the day, it was now Thursday evening. At that point it looked as if the case still had some time to run. It could be expected that Carson would spend some time cross-examining the Commander and Isaacs still had several more witnesses to call including Captain Christian and the promised appearance of Mr Gurrin. It looked as if the hearing had more than another full day to go, which would mean that the court would be called to meet the following Monday, which was bank holiday. At this point the Judge adjourned until the following morning.

13

DENOUEMENT

When the court met again next morning, Friday, everyone, or virtually everyone, expected a day not dissimilar to the three previous ones. However almost at once there was a small surprise. Proceedings should have started with Carson cross-examining Commander Stapleton-Cotton. Instead however the lawyer stood and announced that he understood the Crown wished to call another of their witnesses, Captain Christian, immediately, and so he asked the Judge's permission to postpone his cross-examination of the Commander.

The Captain then went to the witness box and was examined briefly by Avory. Much of what he told the court was by now familiar; he explained how the Commander had reported to him, how he had examined George and Miss Tucker, and had then concluded that George must have been the thief. Some observers in court noticed that there seemed a certain hesitancy and uncertainty in his manner, and this increased when Avory enquired about how quickly he had reached his final conclusion. The Captain replied that he considered the matter both that evening and next morning, implying that he had taken some time and given it careful thought. He also said that he left the final decision what should be done with George to the Admiralty: it was their conclusion and not his.

These claims make interesting reading when compared with the letter which he sent to the Admiralty (page 37). This is not only dated 8th October, but also bears a stamp that it was received at the Commander-in-Chief's Office in Portsmouth on 9th October, so it could not have been the result of careful overnight consideration. The

George Archer-Shee with his mother, his sister Anna and family friend Miss Turner, on the afternoon of the day the case ended.

(*left*) Sir Rufus Isaacs KCMP; (*bottom left*) The Right Hon. Reginald McKenna MP; (*bottom right*) Sir George Lewis

Captain also now seemed to have forgotten the categorical way he recommended George's withdrawal "forthwith" from the College in a way which hardly amounted to "leaving the decision to the Admiralty."

However this was an aspect of the matter which remained hidden; Carson had not seen the original letter, which was one of the documents the Admiralty were so anxious to protect with privilege. Avory finished and sat down; it should next have been Carson's turn to weigh in to the Captain, but watchers in court now realised that dramatic developments were about to take place when instead of getting immediately to his feet he turned and had a hurried *sotto voce* consultation with Isaacs and then merely told the Judge that he had no questions to ask. What was in the wind was soon clear as Isaacs stood and spoke:

> I am glad to tell your Lordship that with regard to the issues of fact, your Lordship and the Jury will not be any further troubled, because as a result of the evidence that has been given during the trial that has been going on now for some days, and the investigation that has taken place, I say now, on behalf of the Admiralty, that I accept the statement of George Archer-Shee that he did not write the name on the postal order, and did not cash it, and consequently that he is innocent of the charge. I say further, in order that there may be no misapprehension about it, that I make that statement without any reserve of any description, intending that it shall be a complete justification of the statement of the boy and the evidence he has given before the Court.

The tensely-hushed court now knew that all the Archer-Shees' and Carson's efforts over the previous twenty-one months were fully and amply repaid; Mr Archer-Shee and Major Martin must both have felt a swell of satisfaction, and so certainly did Carson. George was completely and unquestionably vindicated and Isaacs had used the handsomest and most unambiguous words to say so.

Though not quite everyone in court was so happy at these words. For Captain Christian and Commander Stapleton-Cotton they implied some criticism and withdrawal of support by their superiors, and for Miss Tucker it meant that it was accepted that she had been wrong all along. Isaacs had not quite finished, and he went on:

> Then, my Lord, with regard to the other two questions of fact which are before your Lordship and the Jury for decision, which are issues raised by the Admiralty and involve questions of very important public interest, as your Lordship appreciates, with reference to the discipline and the

administration of the college, my friend accepts my statement, also the statement with regard to the action of the Admiralty to the effect that those responsible for all that has happened were acting under a reasonable and *bona fide* belief in the truth of the statements which have been made to them.

Then after settling a few legal formalities he turned to the question of the postmistress.

> There is just one observation that I should make in justice to Miss Tucker upon whose evidence so much reliance has been placed. It is right to say that it has never been suggested that there was any want of *bona fides* on her part; indeed, the whole cross-examination by my learned friend Sir Edward Carson was directed to showing that notwithstanding her view she might have been mistaken, and had confused two persons. I only want to make it quite clear that, at any rate, there is no suggestion that she was in any way wanting in honesty, so far as she was concerned, in believing the truth of the statement she made.

Isaacs then sat, and with some emotion in his voice Carson stood and spoke:

> My Lord, the complete vindication of George Archer-Shee with regard to the charges that were alleged against him was the object of bringing this petition. That has been entirely achieved by the statement of the learned Solicitor-General on behalf of the Admiralty. That is the first issue of fact. As regards the other two issues of fact, I agree that the responsible persons acted *bona fide* and under a reasonable belief in the statements that were put before them. I also agree on behalf of the Suppliant that as regards Miss Tucker my friend is quite right, that I did direct my cross-examination to show that the lady was mistaken in the evidence she has given. My Lord, of course I regret that the whole action is not now terminated, because the points of law, I suppose, will still remain for argument.

The Judge now said that as they had dealt with the important part of the case he would wait until after the long vacation to hear the arguments on the other matters, which meant mainly the crucial issue that Isaacs had originally raised before Mr Justice Ridley and which, by order of the court of appeal, had been left in abeyance. This would still have to be settled somehow. Discharging the jury Mr Justice Phillimore told them he was glad that an offer they had made to continue sitting through the bank holiday, on the following Monday, was rewarded and they could now go.

To show the way they felt about the whole case some of them immediately climbed out of the jury box in order to cross the court purposefully and shake Mr Archer-Shee's hand. Others in court clustered round Carson to congratulate him as he sat with tears in his eyes; never had any case in which he had been involved affected him more deeply, never had he been happier at an outcome.

Something which went almost unnoticed in all the excitement was that at the crucial moment one person was missing: the centrepiece of it all, George, had not arrived at the court that morning. When he eventually got to the Strand a little later and heard the astonishing news he went straight to Carson's chambers across the road to say his thanks. The lawyer enquired where he had been earlier in the morning and was astonished when George replied that he had been to the theatre the night before and as a result he had overslept that morning.

"What a strange boy you are," observed Carson. "Didn't you feel nervous?"

"When I got into a court of law I knew I would be all right," explained George. "Why, I never did the thing."

"That is a very good way of looking at it," approved Carson.

Meanwhile Major Martin was having a word with the press, who had taken considerable interest throughout and now knew they had a sensation to report.

"We have had many obstacles to overcome during the twenty-one months it has taken us to obtain an investigation," he told the reporters crowding round. "It has simply been a miscarriage of justice which has now been rectified. My brother won the case for himself. His behaviour in the witness box was such that it was impossible not to believe him."

Despite this the sudden end to the case came as a surprise to many people, who seeing how strongly the Crown had fought in the early stages expected the battle to be carried on to the bitter end. The sudden turn around led to many questions being asked, and inevitable suspicions that something had been unearthed which the Admiralty were so anxious to cover up they were prepared to accept the loss of face involved in giving in on the important question whether George was the thief.

The truth is however much simpler. Throughout his legal career Isaacs had never hesitated to tell a client when he thought a case was lost and he should settle for the best terms he could get. This is what he did now. At the end of the third day he had sought out Sir Charles Thomas, who had been observing proceedings, and said quite plainly that on his assessment of the evidence and observation of the jury he was as certain as he could be that they were going to say that George was not the thief; he was supported in this by Avory. In addition he also felt there was a good chance that the jury might be highly critical of the Admiralty and Osborne. Sir Charles immediately got in touch with Mr McKenna. He sent a telegram and wrote a letter*.

27th July 1910

Dear First Lord,
  With reference to my cypher telegram of today.
  The Solicitor-General and Avory both think that the moment has arrived when some settlement of the Archer-Shee case should be affected. They both regard a verdict of acquittal as almost certain, and that the best we can hope for is a finding that the action of the authorities at Osborne and the Admiralty was founded on honest belief, and that there was reasonable ground for such belief.
  Our Naval witnesses are so weak that Counsel consider it is risking an adverse verdict on the latter point to call them, in which case the Admiralty would stand to be shot at both in Press and Parliament, and the results might be very predjudicial.
  The Solicitor-General and Avory are of the opinion that it would be politic to agree to a finding on the facts that the boy did not steal the P.O., conditional on the other side admitting the Admiralty had reason.
  The Solicitor-General would have liked to talk over the position with you, and is very anxious if possible to do so. He will be in his room at the law courts at 10 a.m. tomorrow. If it is impossible for you to come will you wire authority for the Solicitor-General to use his discretion, as action must be taken before the court opens.
  It is of course not certain that the other side will agree to a compromise.

Yours sincerely,
C. Inigo Thomas.

Not everyone concerned was in agreement with this proposed move. There were some bitter argument behind the scenes, and Captain Christian in particular felt strongly. The following morning he penned a hurried letter to Mr McKenna himself.

13, Lowndes Square,
S.W.
July 29th.

Dear Mr McKenna,
  I am quite certain that if you stop this trial now the whole Service will deplore such an action, and the entire country will be against you. I implore you to let it go on and get all our evidence out: personally I would gladly stand or fall by the Jury's verdict and am quite prepared to assume entire responsibility for what was done or left undone at Osborne.

---

* In the McKenna Papers.

The Cross Examination will not be pleasant but the good opinion of my brother Captains and other officers will more than compensate me for a bad hour at the hands of Mr. Carson. Commander Stapleton-Cotton most favourably impressed both Judge and Jury and I have no fear of the result—but in any case I beg and pray you will not stop it now.

> Believe me,
> Yours Very truly,
> Arthur Christian,
> Captain.

Whether this impassioned appeal reached Mr McKenna in time is not clear, but even if it did the First Lord was not prepared to heed it. If the Captain had shown the same thoroughness in the early investigation that he now wanted as the case dragged on to the bitter end then the whole problem might not have arisen. McKenna gave Isaacs authority to use his discretion and so presumably he told Carson what was contemplated before the court opened. This would have enabled Carson to have a word with Mr Archer-Shee, who was doubtless ready to accept a settlement that met in full his purpose in bringing the action. Neither the lawyer nor his client can have realised that by doing so they would allow problems to drag on for a considerable time yet.

It is presumably because of Captain Christian's protest that he was allowed his brief appearance in the witness box, otherwise Isaacs would probably have made his announcement at the start of the day. One of the effects of the sudden end to the case was to deprive Carson of the opportunity of cross-examining Captain Christian or Commander Stapleton-Cotton; it also meant that Mr Gurrin did not make his promised appearance, though on this there is a minor mystery. Mr Gurrin's name is not on the list of witnesses the Admiralty had planned to call, though after Carson's remarks in his opening speech they had probably got in touch with the handwriting expert and asked him to hold himself ready. Had he not appeared Carson would certainly have weighed in with bitter and effective observations on his absence.

If later events were to suggest that Carson and the Archer-Shees too readily accepted the offer of compromise, when it came it seemed to offer all they really wanted; they can hardly have anticipated how official thinking was to develop; McKenna himself had accepted Isaacs's proposal despite a personal conviction, which he always held, that George was the thief.

That afternoon George, with his mother, sister, and a family friend, took a walk in the park where they were photographed by some press photographers. Then, after Mr Archer-Shee had asked the papers to spare his son any more publicity, they left for home at Nailsworth. However, there were a number of people preparing to see that the matter was not immediately forgotten.

14
IMMEDIATE AFTERMATH

The first major reaction this sudden end to the court case came very soon. It was a Friday and so a 'supply' day in the House of Commons when members could raise any question they wished. That afternoon, while George and his family were walking in Hyde Park, Sir Henry Craik, Member for the Universities of Glasgow and Aberdeen, drew Parliament's attention to the matter. When he first mentioned it Mr McKenna was not in the House, but he soon heard it was being discussed and hurried in to his seat on the Government front bench.

In a moderate speech Sir Henry said he did not wish to bring any charge of conscious bias or unfairness against those concerned, and he was sure that the Admiralty would do all in their power to redress what he called a "a very terrible and almost irreparable wrong"; what caused him concern was the way the Admiralty had pleaded privilege at the first hearing and he felt that by doing this they had incurred widespread indignation; he asked the First Lord, now in the Chamber, for an assurance that he would "not again attempt to crush into obscurity and to prevent the light of day being thrown on such a case as this".

He was followed by Sir Henry Dalziel whose aim in speaking was to criticise the use of Mr Gurrin as handwriting expert. He drew attention to his past failures, particularly in the Parnell and Beck cases, and asked for an assurance that the First Lord would use his influence to see that this expert was not put forward in future; it was not fair in trials of this kind that the Government should employ a person who had been shown to be so unworthy to be trusted in matters of this delicate nature.

The question of compensation for George came next, from a Mr Peto, who enquired of Mr McKenna what steps could be taken to wipe out the past two years so that George could return to the Royal Navy if he wished. He paid a tribute to his fellow member, Major Martin, who he knew had devoted every moment of his time when he had not been in the House to this affair for some time past, and he was worried that the case could have shaken public confidence in the whole Osborne system. He did not believe that public opinion would be satisfied unless George was reinstated entirely and there was an assurance that such a case would never recur.

He was supported by a Mr Peel who was highly critical of the investigations at Osborne which he described as "an enquiry which was no enquiry at all". The Admiralty then, he maintained, used the law officers of the Crown to take every technical plea to prevent the facts coming out in public. Then, he continued, when at last they were forced into the open they dare not take the opinion of the jury which, he was confident, would have expressed itself very strongly. He was sure that unless the House could have an assurance that steps would be taken to prevent anything similar happening again he was sure that parents would be prevented from sending their sons into the Navy, and in consequence the service might lose some valuable recruits.

Those four having had their say Mr McKenna intervened. He started by saying that Sir Henry Craik had rightly interpreted the view of the Admiralty when he had said he was sure they would be glad to have the innocence of the boy put on record—he must have had to plant his tongue firmly in his cheek to make this observation—but he soon pointed out that it had also been established that the authorities had acted in good faith and he was also sure the House would be equally glad about this. He then moved on to the use of the demurrer at the outset of the case and it was here he made the appalling remark that "it does frequently happen that private rights have to be sacrificed for the public good"; this observation coming from the mouth of a Liberal politician was particularly remarkable but seems to have been the basis of most of Mr McKenna's thinking on the case.

He then moved on to answer Sir Henry Dalziel's attack on Mr Gurrin. He maintained that the handwriting evidence had been treated as "corroborative evidence only" and explained that the Admiralty had not even intended to call Mr Gurrin as a witness; this is confirmed by the list of proposed witnesses in the Admiralty papers, and Isaacs's contradictory statement in court was presumably a second thought after Carson's opening remarks. Mr McKenna maintained there was no reason for thinking Mr Gurrin an unfair or untrustworthy expert, but just one who had in this case failed, as in many other cases experts could also be wrong.

Dealing with Mr Peto's observations about readmitting George to Osborne he said that after the lapse of two years and the training George would have missed he did not think that this proposal was likely to be raised by either side, and as he did not think Mr Peto was speaking on behalf of the Archer-Shee family he therefore thought it would be better if any such proposal came from them. There is no record that the Archer-Shees ever did consider making such a proposal though there was a good deal of public speculation on the point. After the long delay it would have been impossible for George to catch up on the studies, but also there were undercurrents which made it clear that his return to the service would be very unwelcome.

Mr McKenna's speech did not end Members' interest. Mr Scott Dickinson, who spoke immediately afterwards, observed that it did not seem sound that at Osborne a 13-year-old boy had been accused, and in effect convicted of a theft without his parents being informed. He accepted that the authorities had acted fairly, but they had made a mistake, and there was the possibility of a similar event recurring.

Now, fresh from court, Sir Rufus Isaacs spoke. He said straight away that he could not of course discuss the facts of a particular case in which he had been engaged as counsel, but we wished to say something because of the attack that had been made on the use of the demurrer. He wanted to tell the House at the earliest opportunity that the course he had taken in arguing the point first had not been done on the instructions of the Admiralty; when he had come to the case quite late in the day he had found the plea already on the records and had concluded that it was his duty to argue it at the earliest opportuntity. He had had no consultations with the First Lord or anyone else on the question, and anyway he did not think he could have taken such instructions as it was a matter for a law officer of the Crown. If any blame was to be attributed to anyone he wanted it to be clear it was not to be the First Lord, but to himself.

He explained that he did not think there were any precedents on the matter and so he had felt it highly desirable that a court should pronounce on the question at the earliest possible moment; however when the Court of Appeal had indicated to him that they felt it better that the facts should be tried first he had assented. The legal issues had not been settled, he pointed out, and were still undecided.

He was followed by an Irish Member, Mr Timothy Healey, later first Governor-General of the Irish Free State, who, as was usual for members from across the water, had not got very far before Ireland came into his speech. He recalled that this was not the first case within the previous five years concerning the greatest employer of labour in the three kingdoms, the Crown, and it was a lamentable and parlous state of things if any injustice, no matter how bad, could be committed without there being any right of action. The brogue as the words rolled off his tongue can still be sensed from the printed page today. The problem, he continued, was felt in Ireland in a large number of cases, and it had occurred to him that what was needed was a system akin to that operating in the United States where there was an official whom any person having a grievance of this sort could take action as against any other employer of labour. He knew there were some who took an extreme view of the prerogative of the Crown, but this led them in their treatment of members of the Army, Navy and Civil Service to a return to medieval practices. He wound up his speech, the longest in the debate, with a passionate appeal which started with a reference to the statement by Mr McKenna:

> The First Lord of the Admiralty made one observation with which I respectfully differ. I think it was not well considered. He said that private rights and interests have to be sacrificed for the public good. Of course it is very easy to let fall a phrase like that without seeing its full moment and importance. I think that phrase ought to be reconsidered. I think justice consists in this—and I think the whole British Constitution exists for it—that the humblest and meanest citizen may at the bar of justice and in the King's courts reckon with confidence that absolute justice will be administered. I lay down this proposition that the British sailor and the British soldier and the Irish sailor and the Irish soldier should know with confidence that if any wrong is done them redress will be open to them despite the attitude of high officials of higher authority.

He maintained there were a great many cases of this kind, and asked, almost rhetorically, why they had not been brought forward. He then supplied an answer:

> Because there is a feeling of hopelessness upon the part of those people. They feel it is hopeless to attack this buttressed hierarchy which has set up its claims to immunity for generations. That is the instinctive feelings of all these men. This case, I trust, will lead to proper attention being given to

questions deserving redress and deserving the best consideration of the Law Officers of the Crown, and I do sincerely hope that as justice has been vindicated at this late stage the Government, in order to prevent further injustice arising, will appoint some fair and competent method of trial of such questions.

This cascade of Irish rhetoric was followed by another contribution, a much more modest one, from another Irishman, Admiral Lord Charles Beresford. He opened by saying that as a naval officer he would like to express great satisfaction that justice had been done. He was satisfied that the reports from Osborne had been made in good faith but he found fault with the Admiralty (which at the time was something he did very often) for not assisting the Archer-Shee family more than they did when they made their first approaches; he felt that McKenna's civil servants should have taken more trouble and been more courteous. He then had some very pertinent and true observations about an important point of principle, which had almost been obscured:

> Thieving on a ship or in a regiment is one of the worst crimes that can happen, and for this reason. The men begin to suspect each other. You do not know what may occur. There is irritation and insecurity in barracks or on board ship if there is a thief about; so thus not only has every effort to be made to catch the thief, but you cannot be too careful in getting your evidence thoroughly sifted.

He concluded with the hope that some kind of redress would be made to George, who had suffered so severely and so unjustly for a crime he had not committed. That ended the discussion, and the House moved on to the next matter, a very different question about the Uganda Railway, and Members must have expected this was the last they would hear of the matter, and would perhaps have been surprised to learn that within a year they would have it before them again in a much more lengthy and acrimonious way.

Next day all this was headline news in the papers, though it was forced out of first lead by an even more exciting story which was developing, the chase across the Atlantic of a Dr Harvey Crippen and his girl friend Belle Elmore, in connection with the discovery of Mrs Crippen's murdered body. The factual events of the end of the Archer-Shee trial and the debate in Parliament were well recorded and editorial writers also had their say.

The *Morning Post* indulged in an involved constitutional essay on the whole question of the rights of servants of the Crown, and concluded from this case that it was clear that the powers which the Admiralty clearly had to take away a boy's character without redress were too large. However, rather perversely, the paper also felt that the Captain of Osborne should not have to refer such a question to his superiors at the Admiralty, but should be able to decide himself when one of his charges was no longer suitable for the naval service.

The *Daily Mirror*, which over the previous four days had provided its readers with a fascinating series of photographs, some of them taken in the courtroom, used the opportunity to look at broader issues under the heading "Boys and their Masters". It started with the pertinent if rather obvious observation that this was "one of those cases where nobody was to blame but it certainly could not be said that nobody suffered". All over England, the paper continued, there were hundreds of boys entrusted at immense expense to the keeping of schoolmasters, but many of these masters seemed to think that nothing more was expected of them than to supply bad mutton and fail to teach Latin; when dealing with a serious culprit their usual method was to say "away with him"; they should realise that it was in their power to make bad boys into good men, and more was expected of them than "bad mutton, Greek verbs, and Latin wrongly pronounced."

Immediately under this was a "Thought for the Day", coincidentally a line from Virgil (translated from Latin) which might well have applied to the whole Archer-Shee and Carson approach to the matter: "They can conquer who believe they can".

Back now at Nailsworth, George was deluged with messages of good wishes and congratulations. He spent some time in the local post office sitting alongside a young assistant post master, Percy Evans, who was taking down a continuous stream of telegrams and passing each one over as it came in; George stuffed them all into his pocket. Letters were so numerous that the main sorting offices in London, Birmingham, Liverpool and Manchester were making up special bundles simply labelled "George Archer-Shee, Nailsworth, Gloucester" The boy then had to pay the pennance of writing a mass of 'thank yous'.

Others were also corresponding in the aftermath. A close friend of Carson's, Lady Londonderry, sent a telegram of congratulations to which he replied:

> It has been a great victory and I feel quite tearful over it. I was always convinced of the boy's innocence, and I know it all arose from the blundering suggestion of the officers-in-charge. You should have seen the boy when he came to thank me. He was so frank and honest. My regret is that the Navy will have lost so promising a boy.

Carson also received a letter of profound thanks from Mrs Archer-Shee and he replied to this from the German resort of Bad Homburg, where he had gone for a recuperative rest.

> You are quite right as to my belief in George. Will you please tell him I hope he will always look on me as a friend, and I sincerely hope the whole incident will in the long run turn out to his advantage. He will, I am sure, do well at whatever profession he adopts, and he has the good wishes of everyone. I have come here for a change, being so tired after all the work in the courts.

While all this happy correspondence was going on McKenna also received a letter about the affair in a very different tone. This came from his good friend, the former First Sea Lord, 'Jackie' Fisher.*

> My beloved First Lord,
> An influential friend who begs me not to name him tells me of an unholy alliance between Massingham and Fabian Ware to instigate a campaign against you over the Archer-Shee business, and counsels you to cut the ground from under their feet by some new rules which will obviate a similar case occurring and assume a judicial procedure and to make some offer to Archer-Shee as will cut the ground from under your enemies' feet. As to compensation and apology terms to Archer-Shee you will know best if this is wise advice. Massingham and Co. dread you for the next estimates and the fool Fabian Ware lends himself to them.

To understand this clearly it is essential to know who the two named as forming the "unholy alliance" were. Massingham was editor of a Radical weekly paper *The Nation*, which though it gave considerable support to much of the Liberal Government's activities, was very much on the side of Lloyd-George and his supporters who opposed McKenna's demands for a large slice of the national revenue for the Royal Navy; "the fool" Fabian Ware, as has already been mentioned, was editor of the extreme conservative newspaper *Morning Post*, which could never resist any opportunity to attack McKenna or the Admiralty. The "unholiness" of the alliance between them can best be appreciated when it is recalled that *The Nation* is now merged with the *New Statesman* and the *Morning Post* with the *Daily Telegraph*.

Whether the activities of this alliance led to, or to what extent it even existed is hard to fathom. McKenna did not speedily accept the advice offered to him and there is no sign that the *Morning Post* made any further reference to the matter after its initial editorial until the whole

---

* In the McKenna Papers—The grammar is Lord Fisher's.

question came into the public eye again the following year. Massingham's paper, being a weekly, had more time to mull over the affair and its edition published on 6th August carried a pungent editorial under the heading "The Perils of Bureaucracy" which covered the general issues involved but did not mention McKenna by name.

This started by dwelling on the problems the Archer-Shees had faced in getting George vindicated and went on to make some comparisons with the notorious French Dreyfus affair, which was still quite fresh in the public mind. In this a junior French army officer had been accused of passing secrets to Germany, and convicted on very flimsy evidence. He was only cleared after spending many years on the notorious 'Devils Island' prison and a major feature of this matter had been the hostility and predjudice shown because Dreyfus was Jewish. In its comparison *The Nation* observed that "in the Osborne case no predjudice, social or political, was at work" which confirms that Commander Stapleton-Cotton's anti-Catholic expression had not been retold outside the College.

The editorial continued to make what it considered a key point that "the curse of every service and every hierarchy is the tradition of loyalty to subordinates which is commonly its pride". This was then elaborated into the cynical truism "whenever two or three men are gathered together to rule there grows up amongst them a sense of caste which is the ruin of liberty". The writer then goes on to mention another matter which had caught recent attention, the reported torturing of some Indians by British officials and the way these had been covered up. The summing-up was acrid:

> To do justice, if it is to be done, behind a screen, to cover its good acts with a show of spontaneous magnanimity, but at all costs to exclude the outsider, and to stand shoulder to shoulder in a uniformed and disciplined phalanx against critics and complainants—that is the natural attitude of every hierarchy. The more the functions of our bureaucracies are extended, the graver does the peril to liberty become. There is one way of escape, and one only. It is that all who stand outside the bureaucratic ranks should seize the occasion of some such scandal as these Indian torture cases or this Osborne miscarriage of justice to break the official on whom the working responsibility lies.

From the public point of view that was the end of the matter for a considerable period, and few must have expected ever to hear of it again. Avid followers of court events in the papers had all their attention diverted by the arrest, trial and conviction of Crippen, while those with more serious political interests had plenty else to occupy their attention with the worsening situation in Ireland and the fight between the Liberal Government and the House of Lords reaching its climax. For the time being the young boy, so spiritedly helped by his family and friends, was forgotten.

15

"THE PROPER WAY
OF DEALING WITH
THE QUESTION"

By any reasonable standards that should have been virtually that. There were a few matters still to settle, the way the trial had ended had left some loose ends, with the Judge saying he would deal with outstanding legal points after the long vacation. In practical terms there were three points unsettled: the basic legal question whether the whole petition had been good in law, whether Mr Archer-Shee and George should receive any compensation, and who should pay what costs. In retrospect it seems to have been rather unwise for Mr Archer-Shee and Carson to agree so readily to the Admiralty's offer without at least asking a few pertinent questions on the last two of these topics, but when the proposal had been made it seemed to meet all they had asked for, and they probably did not realise to what an extent the settlement was offered as a means of political escape with little sincerity behind it.

Nothing happened for almost three months after the end of the trial, and in the meantime a minor Government reshuffle had brought promotion for Isaacs, to the top law office of Attorney General. In the middle of October Lewis & Lewis decided the time had come to press the matter, and on the 20th of the month they sent a letter to the Treasury Solicitors enquiring what it was proposed should be done to dispose of the petition as the question of costs and damages were still outstanding. This started a round of correspondence the general tenor of which was soon to have a familiar ring, similar to that of the series of letters with the Admiralty two years before.

Mr Hare of the Treasury Solicitors' Office acknowledged the letter as soon as he received it, saying it would receive "immediate attention". Despite this Lewis & Lewis heard nothing more for ten days, so at the end of the month they sent a curt reminder, saying that they were at a loss to understand why they had heard nothing, and they pressed for the matter to be dealt with without delay. The reply they received, by return, offered the excuse that the Attorney General, whose advice was wanted, had been ill for the past week; however he was expected back in his chambers shortly. Isaacs had just suffered an unpleasant bout of influenza, but he managed to look through the papers as soon as he was well; he then wrote to Mr McKenna, on 2nd November, asking for a chance to discuss the matter as soon as possible.

The same day Lewis & Lewis answered Mr Hare tartly, maintaining that they thought the matter could have been considered by the Admiralty and an answer sent without having to get advice from the Attorney General; this produced no further reaction. The Admiralty were very uncertain what they should do. They still considered that, strictly interpreted, they had the law on their side and so were under no obligation to pay any compensation; privately McKenna and many of his advisers still believed that George was the thief and were not anxious to do more than they need to associate themselves with the court declaration made on their behalf. To some extent they felt that they were the victims of fast legal footwork, perhaps even a plot to discredit the Admiralty and the Government. The letter from Lord Fisher in the last chapter shows that there were probably some who were very happy to use the case to this end.

When after another week Lewis & Lewis had still heard nothing more they sent another curt reminder, but this time they were precipitate, as it crossed in the post with an answer from Mr Hare which read:

9th November

Dear Sir,

    I understand that the request in your letter of 20th ultimo is not made upon any assumption of any legal liability on the part of the Admiralty, in other words that this correspondence is not to be used to prejudice the legal contentions of either side. Upon that basis and with a view to arriving at an agreement disposing of this litigation I am instructed to suggest that Sir Edward Carson should meet the Attorney General to discuss the position.

If therefore you concur in this suggestion perhaps you will be good enough to propose to Sir Edward Carson that he should arrange with the Attorney General for such a meeting.

In the event of no agreement resulting from this correspondence and discussion neither party is prejudiced in his legal contentions.

Yours faithfully,
A. T. Hare

In theory either side could have taken the matter back to court; however for differing reasons neither wanted this. The Admiralty, though confident that they could win on legal technicalities, realised from the public reaction already that such a move would have brought much public criticism, and also they would probably have had a hard time justifying the move to Parliament; they were well aware that the matter had already done them no good. The Archer-Shees and their lawyers knew that they were on shaky legal ground if put to the test so they were equally unwilling to return to law.

However, though this proposal that Carson and Isaacs should get together to try and sort the question out may have seemed reasonable it did not work out. It is recorded in the Admiralty papers that "in consequence of a communication from Carson to Isaacs" no meeting took place. This communication has not survived but it seems to have suggested that the meeting should take place only on the basis of a very large sum of damages and costs, which neither Isaacs nor the Admiralty considered even remotely reasonable.

Meanwhile on the broader political scene the row between the Commons, or to be precise the rather tenuous Government majority in the Commons, and the Lords was getting fiercer. Throughout the summer and autumn Liberal and Conservative leaders had met in conference at Lansdowne House to try and reach some agreement over the future of the Lords, but they failed. There were too many on the Conservative side prepared to "fight to the last ditch", 'ditchers' as they came to be known, who were not interested in anything that suggested compromise, and so those who were more moderate, 'hedgers', could not bring them along with any practical agreement. On the Liberal side too there were those who were so certain it was a battle they could win anyway that they too were not very interested in a settlement. By November the Prime Minister, Asquith, had told the new king that he wished to propose the creation of sufficient number of peers to overwhelm the Conservative majority in the Lords, the number he had in mind was around five hundred. George V was now wrestling with the problem which had clouded his father's final years, and though he was still inexperienced and in the difficult position of working in the shadow of his father's devoutly-remembered memory he handled the situation with skill. He made it clear to Asquith that he could not consent to awarding high honours to so many people who had done virtually nothing to earn them other than giving their support to the right political party, until there had been another General Election. So in November Asquith asked for the dissolution of Parliament in order to go to the country again.

The election took place in dank and chilly December weather and it showed as much as anything that the electorate were getting some-what bored with the whole business; even the most persuasive of partisan orators found it difficult to raise much reaction. In Finsbury Major Martin defended his seat, this time against a Liberal, Mr Felix Rosenheim, Mr Steadman having returned to Union work and barge-building: Liberals and Labour had reached an informal agreement not to stand together in seats where there was a chance that the split vote could throw the seat to the Conservatives.

As elsewhere the votors of Finsbury were not as interested as they had been at the beginning of the year. Major Martin fought another forthright campaign, and his efforts on behalf of his brother had not gone unnoticed in the area. This time when the votes were counted he had retained his seat in a slightly lower poll:

Archer Shee	3335
Rosenheim	2805

He had marginally increased his share of the votes cast, from 52.7 per cent to 54 per cent, which was slightly better than the national average where very few seats changed hands. In the new House of Commons the Liberals' marginal superiority of three over the Conservatives vanished as the two parties tied with 272 seats each; once again the Irish Nationalists and Labour held the balance, and Mr Asquith was forced to continue to trot along with the Nationalists in their demands for Irish Home Rule in return for their continued support over the Budget and the Lords.

When Lewis & Lewis had heard nothing more by the end of January they sent another letter to the Treasury Solicitors; this was more specific than previous communications, and said that as the proposed meeting between Carson and Isaacs had proved abortive they now were instructed to put proposals to end the matter, and they wished for a reply by the end of the week. The proposals were:

1. An undertaking to pay all costs.
2. A personal letter from the First Lord formally withdrawing the original letter and including a generous expression of apology.
3. Compensation of £10,000.

In this last demand they probably overreached themselves, for by the values of the day it was a very considerable sum of money which would have enriched them if all costs were met as well. The immediate reaction from Mr Hare was that the Treasury Solicitors were not yet in any position to give a reply, but would do so as soon as they could. To this Lewis & Lewis replied tartly that it was now six months since George had been completely exonerated and so they asked:

> Surely during this time the Admiralty should have been able to make up its mind as to the proper way of dealing with the question raised in our letter? Further delay is unreasonable and we must ask for a reply at once.

This reply came a week later and it was very negative. It started by stating bluntly that the proposed terms could not be accepted, but the Admiralty were desirous of dealing with the matter "apart from the legal contentions of the Crown which are still open, on the facts found". Then came an offer; but if the Archer-Shees' demand had been excessive then the response was as mean as could be conceived. The Admiralty, the Solicitors said, were willing to pay what are known as the 'taxed' costs of the petition and the preliminary enquiry on all issues, including those where the Archer-Shees had lost; if this was accepted then all litigation would be at an end.

It is hard to believe that this offer was meant to be taken seriously. The term 'taxed' costs refers to the way costs are normally awarded to the winning party in a civil case; he draws up his itemized bill and presents a copy both to the loser and to an official of the Court, known as a Taxing Master. The three then meet and the matter is thrashed out with the Taxing Master deciding what should and what should not be allowed. In Practice there are many expenses which he will disallow and it is estimated that on normal occasions the person collecting costs will receive about half of what he has spent in pursuing the action.

It took Lewis & Lewis a few days to collect their breath and compose a suitable reply. When they did it covered several pages and started by stating that the proposal was in both their client's and their own view entirely inadequate to meet the justice of the case, and they much regretted some effort had not been made to right a cruel wrong. They then went through the whole history of delays they had faced in pursuing the matter and concluded:

> Since July of 1910 no letter of regret has been received from the Admiralty and no offer of compensation for the cruel wrong that has been done both to the boy whose profession has been ruined and to his parents who have gone through a time of the gravest possible distress and anxiety, and at the conclusion of the whole story in answer to what we submit was in every a reasonable proposal we receive a letter from your department written on behalf of the Admiralty in which you offer to pay the 'taxed' costs of the enquiries and litigation which would not, of course, cover even the expenses to which Mr Archer-Shee has been put. Such an offer coming as it does at the end of this long story of injustice is on a par with the general position taken by the Admiralty and seems to us very little short of a declaration of the Admiralty of an intention to make no effort to repair the sad and grievous injury which has been inflicted.

This was greeted with one more of those familiar periods of official silence; nothing was heard in reply for over three weeks. Meanwhile Major Martin and Carson were talking the matter over with some of their fellow Members of Parliament and so knew that if the matter were raised in the House again there would be a sympathetic hearing. They decided now that political action was now the only way forward. The Admiralty may have had some idea of what was afoot, and anyway they were told obliquely by a further letter on 8th March from Lewis & Lewis which stated simply:

> In order that there should be no misapprehension on the matter we are instructed by our client to say that our letter of 13th February closed the correspondence as it concerns you and us, and the matter has now passed out of our hands.

This did not stop the Admiralty from sending a reply. Three days later two letters arrived together at Lewis & Lewis; one was a brief explanatory note saying that the other had already been written when the final notification above had been received, and so they requested that it be passed to their client.

This letter which was several pages long opened by pointing out that the Admiralty had withdrawn all charges against George and repeated the nub of Isaacs's Court statement. It continued by recalling that Carson had accepted that the Admiralty had acted *bona fide* and on reasonable grounds and so:

> . . . while in no way impairing the sympathy due to your client and the regret felt for the mischance by which he suffered so severely, as a complete admission that they are under no moral liability to meet such a claim.

They also denied any legal liability *in toto*. Then they dealt with the claim for £10,000 and here they struck below the belt. They recalled the warning George had received about his poor classroom work and the threat that he might have had to withdraw anyway at the end of term. This, they claimed, showed that he would probably not have made a naval career anyway, and so he had suffered no real loss. To emphasise the point they reproduced the original letter of warning in full. Finally they dealt with the request for an apology; they recalled that at the earliest opportunity, on the day the case ended, the First Lord had expressed his own and the Admiralty's gratification at the vindication of the boy's character; they added that if a letter of withdrawal was required it would be written.

Neither Lewis & Lewis nor the Archer-Shees answered this directly, for they were now moving into the political field. It was out of the question for Major Martin to raise a matter with which he was so closely connected in the House, and he never spoke there about it. A champion had been found in a Conservative Lawyer, Mr George Cave, who was as good a choice as could have been made. In a Parliament where tempers often ran high Mr Cave made his mark by the effective moderation with which he always put forward his case; he was considered to "have a future", and rightly so, for later he became Lord Chancellor.

His first step was to put down a question to the First Lord, asking what steps had been taken or would be taken by the Government to redress, so far as was possible, the wrong done to George, and the pain and loss caused to his family by the unfounded accusation. This came up for an answer in the middle of March, within a week of the last letter from the Admiralty. Mr McKenna replied by merely reiterating the terms of the end of the court case and adding that the Admiralty had offered to pay the taxed costs but they were unable to agree to the demand for £10,000 compensation. Mr Cave came back with a supplementary question enquiring if it was not so that by the charge of theft persisting over many months George had lost any chance of a naval career, and therefore should not the Government, who had made the mistake, offer some kind of compensation. Mr McKenna evaded that direct approach by replying that he did not think this was a convenient moment to open up the case in its entirety as he would have to do for a proper reply, but he suggested that in the course of the debate on the Navy Estimates, which was due shortly, Mr Cave would have an opportunity to give him an opportunity to explain why he thought £10,000 wholly beyond the mark.

However there were a number of members of the House who wanted more than this and felt already that the matter deserved a full-dress Parliamentary discussion. The Opposition leaders were among those who agreed with this, and so next the veteran Conservative, Mr Austin Chamberlain, standing in for his leader Mr Balfour who was away from the House for the day, gave notice that a motion would be put down at an early date so that the case could be discussed apart from the estimates.

Lord Charles Beresford then came in to enquire if the Admiralty had offered any expressions of regret over the the incident. Mr Mc-Kenna's answer came as something of a surprise to those listening who were fully acquainted with the case. Yes, he replied, if the Noble Lord had followed the case in the courts and recalled his later statement in the House he would know that both the Attorney General had expressed regret at the end of the case and he himself had done so at the earliest opportunity in the House. The surprise which some hearers greeted this was because they could recall no expression of regret at any stage, any such sentiments had been conspicuously absent. They had certainly not been any part of Isaacs's statement, unreserved though it was, and in his statement to the House Mr McKenna had been too anxious to get on to defending his department to have time for them.

The final supplementary came from Mr Peel who asked if his understanding was correct that the Admiralty was proposing to pay no compensation. Mr McKenna denied this but he added that as there would probably now be a debate inside the House he should be glad for guidance on the question; his own present opinion was that when all the facts were known it would be held it was not a case for compensation. With that the matter rested until it was time to discuss the Naval Estimates, early the following month; then everybody would see if McKenna's view was the one which would be generally taken.

16

PARLIAMENT'S GUIDANCE

Before the matter was discussed by Parliament again Lewis & Lewis got together all the correspondence between them and the Admiralty and the Treasury Solicitors and had it printed as a pamphlet. This inevitably showed how often they had had to press for replies, and also exactly what had been said in answer to the request for compensation; it was all there including the letter warning about George's classroom work, so nothing adverse was omitted. This was circulated to interested Members of Parliament and the press so that they could see for themselves; the pamphlet contained no comments.

Several newspapers carried summaries and reprinted the key letters. Mr Archer-Shee also wrote to *The Times* which summarised his letter in a report the day before the debate. He pointed out that the offer to pay taxed costs had only been made on 8th February though correspondence on this had started as early as the previous 20th October. He also said he could find no trace anywhere of the apology which Mr McKenna claimed had been made. The claim for compensation, Mr Archer-Shee emphasized, was not only based on his son being dismissed without fair trial but also because all efforts to obtain a fair trial had been frustrated until the Admiralty had been forced by the Court of Appeal. He concluded:

> . . . all the time the Admiralty, with callous persistence, kept my son branded as a thief and a forger, and but for the action of the Court of Appeal he would have remained so branded—by the Admiralty—for the rest of his life.

152

This gave the Admiralty some idea of the criticism they would face when the matter came up in the House on Naval Estimates Day, Thursday 6th April. They and the Treasury Solicitor were anxiously looking round for some reply; they were getting almost paranoiac on the issue and started to suspect a long-standing plot. A letter from the Treasury Solicitor to McKenna's office dealing with what it calls "statements made by the Archer-Shee party to the newspapers" tries to refute them:

> The dates I think show that approximately some thirty weeks are attributable to the Petitioners, and that no unnecessary delay occurred on the part of the Admiralty. The aim of the solicitors all through was evidently to manufacture charges of delay; for instance, at the end of October and beginning of November 1908 they were complaining that they were receiving no reply to their communications when they knew that during the whole time they were in semi-official communication with Lord Desart upon the matter. On 1st December 1909 they themselves asked for ten days further time, while on 19th April 1910 they wrote to ask that the case should stand over until after the long vacation, that is until the next sittings, and after this the Law Courts Branch asked for an early appointment to agree correspondence as the Solicitor General was anxious to bring the case on.

The allegation that Lewis & Lewis were anxious to manufacture charges of delay all through is clearly absurd; it seemed to be forgotten that the discussion with Lord Desart was confidential, and also that Sir George himself had been in semi-retirement at the time and so was not in constant contact with his partners at the office; at this stage he had retired completely and he died at the end of the year. What remained unmentioned was that it had taken a full month before the other two lawyers, Poole and Elliot, had managed to get to Osborne and make enquiries, a period during which the evidence must have got a bit 'cold'. How anyone could suggest on reading the letters that they were aiming to manufacture charges of delay is almost beyond belief; the request for extra time, not very much, and to stand the case over had only been made when the matter was already a year old and it was far too late to consider such remedial action as getting George back to Osborne. Even if the case had got to court a few months earlier it could have had very little effect on the outcome, and the solicitors also seemed to have forgotten that they themselves asked at one point for 'extra time'.

The document quoted above goes on to complain about the "delay" before Lewis & Lewis wrote after the final trial to enquire what should be done to dispose of the matter. They had waited almost three months though it might well be felt that in the circumstances it should have been the Admiralty's task to make the first move; it was clear that even after the three months the Admiralty and the Treasury Solicitors had given no thought to the matter and had no idea what to do about it. The one awkward question that could be asked of the Archer-Shees was if their demand for £10,000 and all costs was not unreasonable; it may even have been a move to force another Commons debate. However the Admiralty could easily have countered with a more reasonable offer.

By the time the Commons debate was due many members had had a chance to read the letters and look carefully at the matter: many felt that Mr McKenna was going to have to deal with a lot of awkward questions. The procedure which had been followed to allow the matter to be discussed was a motion, put down by Mr Cave, to reduce the salary of the First Lord of the Admiralty by a hundred pounds, which is one of those delightful British parliamentary traditions, and the accepted way of criticising the conduct of an individual minister.

The day of the debate Parliament assembled at a quarter to three and started with the usual period of question time. Immediately this was over, and before the naval supply debate had even started, a Labour member, Mr O'Grady, was on his feet: he had clearly developed no sympathy for the Archer-Shees and was not happy that the matter was going to be discussed at all. The attitude of the Labour Party to individual injustice by official bureaucracy always tends to be mixed and limited: as the believers in a vast state machine, and the philosophy that the "man in Whitehall is always right", they are prone to support the state machine against the individual; also, and this was important in this matter, their sympathy for wrongs against an individual tends to be confined to individuals from the 'working class'. Had George been a victimised Trade Unionist then Mr O'Grady would have taken a very different line, but he and his party colleagues had been rather incensed by the size of the demand made in compensation.

Immediately question time was finished Mr O'Grady asked the Speaker if he was aware that the purpose of the motion put down by Mr Cave was to bring the Archer-Shee case before the house, whether it was not a fact that there had been contact between the front benches on this, and if Mr Speaker himself had been consulted. It would, Mr O'Grady felt, cause some time to be spent on a minor matter compared with other pressing matters which needed to come before the House.

The Speaker replied that he did not follow Mr O'Grady; he explained that the Prime Minister had offered a day for discussion of the matter and this was the day; was there anything improper in such a motion being put down? Mr O'Grady repeated his enquiry, whether Mr Speaker "as guardian of the liberties of private Members" had been consulted; the Speaker replied that it did not concern him at all. It is Parliamentary practice that when a supply debate starts the House 'goes into Committee' and the Speaker leaves the Chair, his place is taken by the chairman of the Committee of Ways and Means.

Despite this Mr O'Grady continued by enquiring if, when the debate started, this matter was discussed, would it not be distinctly out of order as it was not a question of supply but of compensation to an individual. The Speaker replied that this was not a matter for him but for the chairman of the Committee of Ways and Means. Mr O'Grady persisted; he formally raised a point of order because, he explained, he felt some protest should be made against the course of business that day; he asked if he might move an adjournment so that business he wished to be discussed could be discussed. This, he explained, concerned the forthcoming coronation of King George V, due on 22nd June; Mr O'Grady believed there would be many hundreds and thousands of men and women and children who would be required to rejoice at this when they were starving. The Speaker replied that this was not a matter which could be raised at this point and added that if Mr O'Grady objected to a reduction in the First Lord's salary he should vote against the motion. Amid laughter Mr O'Grady replied that he did not object and was told that then he could vote in favour.

Next Mr O'Grady started to move formally his urgent motion about feeding for the coronation but the Speaker interrupted before he had finished to enquire how something that was not due until 22nd June could be so urgent; Mr O'Grady replied that if the hungry were to be fed in time arrangements would have to start immediately. A feeling may have begun to permeate to some parts of the House that the Honourable Member was invoking the ancient and well-tried Parliamentary privilege of making an honourable fool of himself. At this point the Labour veteran Mr Keir Hardie came to his rescue by explaining that while he himself did not minimise the importance of the particular incident they feared it might exclude discussion of general naval questions. The Speaker once more reiterated that this was a matter for the chairman of the Committee of Ways and Means and explained to Mr O'Grady that the proper time to raise his coronation feeding point was when the salary of the President of the Local Government board was under discussion. The House then turned briefly to some general questions about future business, dealt in the absence of the Prime Minister, who was sick, by young Mr Winston Churchill.

The Debate proper started at around four o'clock. The Speaker left the Chair, and the Chairman of the Committee, Mr Emmott, took his place. He had only just done so when Mr O'Grady was on his feet again, this time to enquire if he was entitled to move that they "report progress", a motion which, if allowed, would have meant that they would have gone straight past present business. The Chairman told him this was not possible as it was the day allotted for the Navy estimates. Immediately another Labour Member, the future party leader and Prime Minister Ramsay Macdonald, was up to say that he understood the whole of the day was going to be taken up with what he described as an attempt at "what is practically to blackmail the Treasury". This provoked outraged cries of "Withdraw" and a request from the Chair that Mr Macdonald put his point with as little controversy as possible. Mr Cave claimed the expression was a breach of order and asked that it should be withdrawn immediately; the chairman would not accept that it was out of order though he did agree that the observation was "objectionable": Mr Macdonald then unhesitatingly withdrew it and explained that the point worrying him was that the whole of the day was to be given to the matter to the exclusion of other business; the chairman assured him that though he considered they should spend the first part of the day on it he understood that those concerned did not necessarily want to carry on with the matter for the whole of the day.

Mr Cave then rose and formally moved the reduction of the First Lord's salary. He told the House he made no apology for bringing the matter forward, in part at least because of the First Lord's invitation to do so, and in view of Mr Macdonald's observations he emphasized that he did so entirely on public grounds; he knew nothing of Mr Archer-Shee personally and he had had no communication either with him or his son. He thought that on public grounds attention should be called to the case, and whether Mr O'Grady accepted this or not did not concern him.

He would not re-open the case but he only wanted to call attention to certain facts. He went over the details briefly and said that there were three points in particular which required explanation. First he wanted to know how such a grave charge could be brought against someone without them being given an opportunity to defend themselves. He then explained to those members who had raised persistent points of order that he knew Mr Archer-Shee was not a rich man and the case had cost him a great deal.

His second point was a more general one: how it was that when so serious a charge had been made there was no process whereby the facts could be publically examined; if there really was no such procedure then he felt one should be invented. Thirdly he was concerned about the way the Crown had used the demurrer; why was it, he enquired, that the "old tradition that whenever a subject wanted access to the courts of the country and desired a decision of a jury the Crown did what it could to help" had been forgotten? He pointed out how the matter had had to be taken to the court of appeal, and then eventually after George had been cross-examined by one of the ablest Counsel at the bar it became apparent to the Admiralty, as it had been apparent to others for some months already, that no jury in England would come to a verdict adverse to the boy. Since then he had learnt that George's fellows at Osborne had always believed him innocent.

Mr Cave then recalled how in the earlier debate in the House Members had said that they were content to leave settlement to the generosity of the Admiralty; where Government departments had erred it had always been the practice if possible to redress the wrong, but on this occasion nothing at all had been offered so eventually Mr Archer-Shee had put in this claim for £10,000. He agreed that this was large, and that it was probably too large, at which Mr McKenna intervened to say this was the only point of difference. If so, returned Mr Cave, then Mr McKenna should have offered a smaller sum. He thought however that what was really wanted was not so much money as some definite act which would mark the fact that the charge had been finally withdrawn. He considered that a formal expression of regret should have been sent, together with an offer of substantial compensation.

Instead all that had been offered were 'taxed costs', which would have meant that Mr Archer-Shee would have to pay a considerable part of the expenses out of his own pocket; this was most unfortunate and required explanation. Mr Cave next moved to the excuse offered for not paying any compensation, the warning letter which had been sent about George. The suggestion seemed to him to be that because George had not been very diligent in his studies he should not mind being charged with theft; he did not think this suggestion would be repeated in the House.

To sum up, Mr Cave said, he would like to know whether boys going to such schools as Osborne could not be protected against ill-considered charges of this kind: he understood that this was not the only such case for he had heard of a somewhat similar incident at Dartmouth. He hoped that Mr McKenna had now had time to reconsider the matter, and would make a right and generous offer. He had brought the matter forward not to appeal to any particular party in the House, and he felt confident that if everybody was free to speak his mind there were few who would not think that something should be done to put the matter to rights.

Mr McKenna opened his reply by paying tribute to the "moderate and complete" manner in which Mr Cave had presented his case; he had not, he said, a shadow of complaint against a single word which had been uttered and indeed he was glad of an opportunity to explain certain matters. A strong trace of smug complacency was to run through the First Lord's speech. He was aware, he said, that there was a notion in certain quarters that the Admiralty had been vindictive and desired to conceal traces of its action to prevent justice being done; but the one desire of all concerned had been to get at the truth. He had an administrative duty, he maintained, if he believed a boy guilty of such a charge as had been levelled against George, to remove him from the college. He then went into a long-winded digression about the duty of those at the College and came back to the familiar refrain that though the charge had now been withdrawn by the Admiralty it had also been agreed that the Admiralty had acted on a reasonable belief of the truth of statements made to them.

"If a man holds a reasonable belief then it is his duty to act on it," he insisted.

He then turned to details and explained the way the first handwriting report had been obtained. He claimed that as soon as he saw the papers he recognised at once the terrible infliction such a matter would bring both on the boy himself and his parents, so he looked for any evidence that would enable him to say the Captain of Osborne had been wrong. He noticed that there was no report of any handwriting comparison—Commander Stapleton-Cotton's amateur effort had not been mentioned—so he decided to have one made; he was well aware that handwriting experts were often wrong when they said a document was written by a particular individual, but they were not so often wrong when they said it had not been written by some individual. When he sent the postal order to Mr Gurrin he had done so in the hope that he would be told that the signature had not been written by George. This, he explained, was the reason for the delay between the first report of the theft and the final letter requiring George's withdrawal. This explanation stands up to close examination, though it does not satisfy the complaint that Mr Archer-Shee had been kept in ignorance while it was all going on.

Mr McKenna next revealed that as a result of the case he had made some amendments to the Osborne regulations. What he believed caused most mischief on such occasions was when a charge was made, investigated and became a matter of public notoriety before the Admiralty had ever heard of it. He had now issued instructions that no public enquiry which could lead to any publicity or to a cadet being removed from the college should take place until both the cadet's parents and the Admiralty had been informed. In this case, he claimed, the Captain of Osborne had inherited a system and had acted strictly in accordance with regulations in existence at the time.

He next turned to the criticism that the Admiralty had been tardy when first approached by Lewis & Lewis. This he justified by explaining about the meeting between Lord Desart and Sir George Lewis; Lord Desart had first communicated with Sir George six days after the first letter and they had met three days later. The whole complaint was based on a misunderstanding, he maintained, and he had no doubt that Mr Cave was hearing this for the first time.

"Why?" Mr Cave wanted to know, and Mr McKenna elaborated by explaining that while Lord Desart and Sir George had been in touch another partner in the firm who knew nothing about the matter noticed that the unanswered letters and initiated the reminders. He made no mention of the confidential nature of the meeting which had precluded it being discussed with anyone but Carson, not even Mr Archer-Shee had been aware of it, and the First Lord was content that he had offered an adequate explanation. He was getting more and more self-righteous about the conduct of his department as he continued:

"What did we do next? I do not suppose there is any precedent for such action as ours in the whole course of experience of Public Departments."

One Member, Earl Winterton, was unable to resist the temptation to greet this pomposity with a cynical "Hear, hear".

The unprecedented action, Mr McKenna explained in hurt tone, was allowing the Archer-Shees' legal representatives to make their own enquiries at Osborne; after this, Lewis & Lewis had sent him a long report which he had read carefully, but he had not felt it justified him in refusing to accept the statement of the Captain of the college. He then looked around for someone to investigate afresh and selected Mr Acland who he felt was particularly well qualified for the task. Mr Acland, he recalled, had been Judge Advocate to the Fleet for some time, since 1904, he was legally experienced and his job had made him used to querying official decisions, so he should if anything have had a bias towards the defendant.

A Mr O'Shaughnessy intervened to ask if the handwriting expert had declared the handwriting on the stolen postal order to be the same as George's; Mr McKenna parried this by saying he was not anxious to bring out anything that might minimise the effect of the withdrawal of the charge. He then turned to the use of the demurrer at the first trial; this was a matter for the Law Officer, he maintained, but he did not feel that justice had been done to Isaacs for giving way so generously in the Court of Appeal.

Next he came to the use of the 'warning' letter as a reason for not paying any compensation. He got off on the wrong foot by implying that Mr Cave had accused him of inventing or trumping up the charge; Mr Cave denied strongly that he had suggested any such thing. Mr McKenna then amended his statement because, he claimed, he wanted to be "perfectly fair"; the fact, he said, was that this letter had originally been with the papers on the case, but when they had crossed his desk on their way to the solicitors he had personally withdrawn it, as he did not think it affected the issue to be tried, and he had never intended to use it until the sum of £10,000 compensation had been mentioned. Was such a large sum reasonable, he wanted to know, when it was more than a naval officer would receive if he retired after 30 years' service. Such warning letters were not idle threats, he maintained; in the year 1908 they had been sent to the parents of 27 Osborne cadets, and of these boys 12, slightly less than half, had in the end been withdrawn, so on this evidence George's chance of making a naval career was only a half-chance.

Defending his offer of 'taxed costs' only he replied that if this was not satisfactory then he wanted to know just how much was required, for surely a bill of costs had been rendered by now. He was greeted with some sympathetic noises from his own benches when he stated that one thing he did not want to do was to give a blank cheque of public money to any firm of solicitors, however eminent. He closed by maintaining that he had only acted throughout with a desire to do his duty, and in accordance with what he believed was his duty; he then sat down, seemingly satisfied that he had persuaded the House of his view.

However it quickly became clear that he had not achieved this. He was followed by Mr Scott's pupil, the already-mentioned young firework, F. E. Smith, who opened by saying he would attempt to retain the attention of the Committee by following the example, method, and tone of those who had just spoken. He first drew attention to the high character with which George had gone to Osborne and he considered it a grave error of judgement that the boy's parents had not been notified during the ten days after the first accusation. He then described the interview between Sir George and Lord Desart as an extraordinary way for the Admiralty to conduct important business and he thought also that the Admiralty's refusal to show the report by the Captain of Osborne gave the cause for the gravest possible complaint; he wanted to know where this report was now, for it could not be contended that there was still anything confidential about the case. Another aspect he attacked was the enquiry by Mr Acland. He knew Mr Acland well and respected him, but even the most competent and humane judge that ever lived was wholly unable, he maintained, to sift and investigate a charge like this unless he had the assistance of those concerned and both sides were represented at the enquiry; yet this vital representation had been denied. He read out the court letter of refusal from the Admiralty and added that he thought Mr McKenna would not now defend this.

On the question of costs he suggested that Mr McKenna should have offered to pay what are known in legal terminology as actual costs 'between party and client'; these would also have been subject to examination by a Taxing Master who would have prevented them being excessive. This expressions covers a much more generous scale of costs which are occasionally awarded to the winning party in a civil case when the judge feels that the looser has been very unreasonable and put his opponent to unnecessary expense; they cover anything that is at all necessary for the conduct of the case. Mr Smith finished by referring to the claim for compensation, while he thought £10,000 might be on the high side he considered that the Government should not be mean.

As he sat down Isaacs rose. What the Attorney General had to say was something of an elaboration of the speech he had made in the earlier debate, once again he carefully avoided entering into detail of a case in which he had acted, but he wanted to defend again and in more detail his use of the demurrer. George, he maintained, had been an officer in the Royal Navy when at Osborne, and although he had searched thoroughly he could find no precedent at all anywhere for allowing an officer in the King's service to bring a case into a court of justice.

Carson intervened to point out to Isaacs that whether a cadet was an officer or not was one question not settled by the action. Isaacs replied that there was no doubt about it, at which Lord Charles Beresford interposed to point out that even so he could not claim a Court Martial, which was every other officer's right. This is the point which has always been the main ground for criticism of Isaacs's action in resort to the demurrer at the beginning of the case; even though he was right in claiming that there were no precedents for an officer to take a case to a court of law there was also no exact precedent for this particular case, of an officer who could take his case to no other tribunal. There were special and unusual circumstances that would have let a law officer take a different view and allow a break with precedent.

Isaacs replied to Lord Charles with some involved legal arguments and also the claim that he had actually been criticised by some lawyers for giving way in the court of appeal. All this had gone on for some time when Mr Alfred Lyttelton interposed to enquire whether they should spend so much time on a point of law; Mr O'Grady assented vigorously with the observation that it was a "damned scandal"; Mr Cave objected to this phrase as "unparliamentary" but the chairman had his convenient deaf ear turned when the remark was made and replied that he had not heard it. Mr O'Grady continued protesting about the case being tried over again by lawyers in the House, but the chairman told him he could only do this when he caught the Chair's eye; Mr O'Grady however had had enough and he stalked angrily from the Chamber.

Mr Lyttelton continued, and after covering once again the complaint about the use of the demurrer he suggested that Mr McKenna's new regulations for Osborne made no clear provision for representation at enquiries. He then pointed out that the expressions of regret which Mr McKenna had claimed at question time three weeks before were not to be found anywhere in the record of either the court proceedings or Parliament. Mr McKenna admitted he had made a mistake and amended it by now making "the fullest and most unqualified expression of regret" to both father and son.

Two more Members, Mr W. F. Roach and Mr Norman Craig, both expressed the view that generous costs and compensation were due, and by this time Mr McKenna could not help being aware that this was the general feeling of the House. He busily held some private consultations and then announced that Carson and Isaacs had agreed to meet together with an impartial third party to settle the matter—it was hoped that the third man would be the distinguished Admiralty lawyer Lord Mersey—the trio would form an arbitration panel to make a recommendation to the First Lord.

This seemed to settle the issue but there were a few more members with something to say. Mr P. J. Power was anxious to add a word for the particular reason that he was an old Stonyhurst boy. He told the House he had visited his old school recently and was impressed with the way everyone there had complete faith in George. After this Mr Cave endeavoured formally to withdraw his motion, but a Mr Moreton objected: he wanted to use the occasion to say something about the general question of the misuse of Crown privilege, but he was soon wandering so far away from the issue at hand that he was brought back to earth by the Chairman.

Then Lord Charles Beresford had his go. 'Charlie B' really had the bit between his teeth, for he must have watched with great pleasure the discomfiture of his arch-foe McKenna and he was quite unable to resist the opportunity to add to it: he succeeded more than anything in bringing the matter to an end with a touch of comic relief. He first came back to the expression of regret for it was he who had asked the supplementary question which had received Mr McKenna's misleading answer. Mr McKenna explained to him that on that occasion he had been answering on the spur of the moment without a chance to consult the papers; Lord Charles thought this merely showed how inaccurate the First Lord was. He then spoke about boys who had received a 'warning' such as George, and he raised a good laugh when he said he would not refer to himself, but to his brothers, and there had been no better boys than they, yet they had together been warned a total of forty times; he would always have greater respect for boys who had received such a warning. He was clearly thinking of those high-spirited youths who get into scrapes in their young days but make a very positive contribution to the world as they mature; the armed services are full of examples.

Lord Charles soon wandered on to other naval matters where he could also 'have a go' at McKenna, including the inevitable question of the Dreadnoughts, and that proved to be an end to the main discussion. It was now just after seven in the evening, so George's problem had occupied the House for a full three hours. All that was left was for Carson and Isaacs to get together with Lord Mersey, and for McKenna and the Admiralty to contemplate the rough ride they had received.

The trio given the task of settling the matter were unable to get together for several weeks: it was almost the end of May when eventually they met. What facts and statements they considered is not recorded, but early in June Lord Mersey sent the Admiralty their joint recommendations that Mr Archer-Shee should be paid compensation of £3,000 and allowed costs of £4,120, and that this should bring the whole matter to an end.

The Admiralty still managed one final piece of bloody-minded awkwardness. Though presumably both Mr Archer-Shee and Lewis & Lewis heard informally from Carson how the matter had been settled, they had still received no official communication by the middle of July. The thought may have crossed their minds that even at this stage somehow the Admiralty were going to try and find an excuse to duck. Lewis & Lewis now wrote the sort of letter that must have become almost automatic to them; they told the Admiralty that they were most surprised at having heard nothing and requested an immediate reply.

At the Admiralty and the Treasury Solicitors' Office it was recalled that the last communication they had received from Lewis & Lewis was the letter which said that "the matter as far as it concerns you and us is now closed", and this was dug out. The reply Lewis & Lewis received after a few days opened therefore on a note of surprise, that they should be interested in the question at all; it went on condescendingly to say that for the information of Mr Archer-Shee the Admiralty had received the Mersey/Isaacs/Carson report and various matters arising from it were "under consideration".

This was particularly unfortunate as the letter from Lewis & Lewis had arisen indirectly out of an informal query Isaacs had made to them about who should receive the money: the Admiralty did not realise this until after their letter was posted. To give credit where it is due these particular actions were not Mr McKenna's personal responsibility, and as soon as the papers crossed his desk he did what he could to expedite matters by writing "This is Urgent" along the bottom. The Admiralty had one practical matter to sort out before they made the payment, they had to clear with the Treasury which vote, or source of funds, should be used. However this was soon settled and Mr Archer-Shee sent a formal letter to Isaacs authorising payment to Lewis & Lewis, who duly received the cheque.

How far Mr Archer-Shee's expenses were covered is not clear. Certainly £4,120 was a fair sum of money and was probably something near to the 'party and client' costs mentioned in Parliament; however even in those days legal costs could be very high and top counsel such as Carson had briefs marked as high as £1,000 a day. It is doubtful if Sir Edward went as high as this in a case about which he felt so strongly but he would certainly have been entitled to fair reward for his invaluable work, as would Mr Scott, Mr Hoffgaard and Lewis & Lewis. For the Crown the situation was easier. Those who prepared the case, the Treasury Solicitors, were all Crown servants, and Isaacs presented the case in court as part of his duties as Solicitor General. In him the Crown had a most able lawyer very much on the cheap, for his salary was only a fraction of what he had been earning in private practice at the bar, which his biography claims went as high as £27,000 a year at this time.

One small loose end remained untied. No formal letter withdrawing the charge was ever sent either to George or his father; Mr McKenna felt that what he had said in the House of Commons was adequate and there was no need to put anything further in writing. Mr Archer-Shee did not pursue this, for in the final account all his efforts had been fully vindicated, and his youngest son could make his way in the world with an unblemished character.

17

FINISH

George completed his education at Stonyhurst, leaving early in 1912. The records there suggest he was a good average boy, he got into the football First Eleven in his last year, but the activity that attracted him most was debating; his name appears in the records of most meetings of the college Debating Society where he usually followed family tradition by taking a 'Conservative' line; however on one occasion, when the value of circumstantial evidence in deciding the fate of a convicted murderer was being discussed, he, not surprisingly, was aware of the dangers of such circumstantial evidence.

Stonyhurst was one of the sufferers from the case; the Admiralty had been furious at the way George was so readily accepted back there and at the frequent reaffirmation of belief in his innocence by the staff and boys. For some time the college authorities knew that any of their boys who tried to enter the Navy stood a slim chance, and when in 1914 one by the name of Slattery did insist he wanted to get into the service the headmaster warned his family that he would be most unlikely to make it direct from Stonyhurst. He was therefore transferred to another school, the Jesuit Wimbledon College, as a day boy on the pretext of a minor illness for a couple of terms. This way he was accepted, made a distinguished career and retired Rear-Admiral Sir Matthew Slattery.*

When George left school he decided to try his father's world of finance, and also to travel. He went to the United States where he joined the Wall Street firm of Fisk & Robinson and started to learn

---

* Information in personal letter to the author.

166

the business. His father by this time was feeling his years and his health had suffered under the strain of the long battle. Early in 1913 he paid a visit to his elder son, Major Martin and his family, who were living at Sunninghill in Berkshire and while there he collapsed and was taken to hospital in Windsor. He died on 27th March of a combination of heart disease and pneumonia: he was 66.

Major Martin continued his parliamentary career where he made his mark as an able back-bencher, through he never reached Government office. He was particularly active in criticising the members of the Liberal Government involved in what was known as the 'Marconi Scandal', which arose out of allegations that some ministers had profited by inside knowledge about the award of a contract for an Empire chain of radio stations. A principal among these was Sir Rufus Isaacs, whose brother Godfrey was a director of the American Marconi Company; however subsequent investigation cleared the Ministers of the most sinister allegations made against them even if some of them, including both Isaacs and Lloyd George, had been 'unwise' at least.

In 1918 the Major's name appeared in the Honours list and he became Major Sir Martin Archer-Shee. Unfortunately in 1922 there was some redrawing of parliamentary constituency boundaries which resulted in the enlargement of the Finsbury division; the new sector contained a heavy preponderance of Labour voters, sufficient to swamp Major Martin's supporters at the next election. His political career was now over despite occasional suggestions that he should stage a come-back. About this time he started his other protracted battle with authority, with the Inland Revenue, whom he challenged over the tax assessment of his wife's inherited income from the United States; this fight lasted fourteen years and ended in the House of Lords with a victory for the Major; he died soon afterwards in 1935 at 63.

The political events which formed the background to the Archer-Shee case continued to simmer for some time. The Commons and the Lords managed to sort out their differences with the peers accepting a curtailment of their ancient rights. In Ulster Carson's valiant championship of George had been watched with admiration and was an important factor in helping him, as a Dubliner, to be rapidly accepted as the champion of the six counties. He continued to battle on their behalf both in and out of Parliament so vigorously that some opponents muttered "treason"; certainly he and others were prepared to go to almost any lengths to prevent Ulster being ruled from Dublin. The situation was not far from civil war when the First World War intervened and eventually when this was over the divided Ireland solution was achieved. For his part in this Carson has sometimes been branded as 'anti-Catholic'. This charge never stood up to serious examination and his championship of George should be enough to kill it completely.

When in the middle of the First World War Lloyd-George formed his coalition Government, Carson held McKenna's old office of First Lord of the Admiralty for a short while; though he was there when the much-delayed decision to introduce the convoy system to give better protection to merchant ships against U-boats was finally taken and is entitled to some of the credit for this, the job was not really his *forte* and he only stayed a few months. When not active in politics he continued to practise at the bar, though *Rex v. Archer-Shee* proved to be the last of his courtroom clashes with Isaacs. Both the great advocates died within a short space of each other in 1935, and the warm regard they had for each other, despite their frequent legal opposition and political difference is shown by the way they exchanged messages enquiring about each other as they neared their ends. Both died Peers of the Realm, Isaacs as the Marquess of Reading, and Carson with a non-hereditary Law Lord title, Lord Carson of Duncairn. His first wife died in 1912 and in 1914 he remarried very successfully a much younger woman, Miss Ruby Frewen, who had admired him from afar for some time, in particular for his handling of the Archer-Shee Case.★ However Carson's heir, a son by his first wife, had not made a success of his life; he got into the hands of moneylenders and all his family knew of him was that he was working as a marker in an Australian Billiard Hall, so his father declined an offer of a hereditary title which would have passed to him, and he also sponsored a successful Bill in Parliament to curb some of the more rapacious activities of moneylenders. His second son, Walter, who had been at Osborne and had reached the rank of Commander in the Navy, shot himself over a girl, and his daughter died from drugs, and so his first family was not a

---

★ This is presumably the rather slender origin of the 'romantic' episode in the Rattigan play involving the cadet's sister. Miss Frewen was however no relation of the Archer-Shee family; George's albeit very pretty sister Anna was only in her teens at the time. Major Martin's last surviving sister, Winifrede, died when nearly 90 early in 1972, after the author of this book had had a chance to talk to her. At the time George went to Osborne both she and her elder sister Mary were enclosed in a convent, where they gave their lives to teaching. A newspaper report when Winifrede died implying she might have been the romantic interest is therefore nonsense.

success. He did not live long enough to see his and Ruby Frewen's son, Edward, enter the House of Commons for seven years as the 'baby of the House' in 1945.

Despite McKenna's ham-fisted handling of the case he is generally rated as having been a good First Lord, mainly because of his under-standing of the needs of the Navy at the time, his good relationship with the Sea Lords and his early appreciation of the German danger. However by the end of 1911 there had been enough criticism for the Prime Minister to decide it was time for a change, and a reluctant McKenna swapped jobs with the Home Secretary, Winston Churchill. At the Home Office his main headache was that monstrous horde of women, the Suffragettes, and he earned the undying opprobrium of all feminists by the firm stand he took against them, particularly his method of dealing with prison hunger strikes; his ingenious solution to these was what was nicknamed the 'Cat and Mouse' Act, which provided for the temporary release of those who starved themselves: when they had recovered their health they were recalled to complete their sentence. At the end of the First World War the Liberal Party went into rapid decline and McKenna left politics for the City where he became a distinguished Chairman of the Midland Bank; his speech at each general meeting became a key annual attraction for the financial world. He rates as one of those considerable political figures who "might have been Prime Minister" but who never quite made it; he died during the Second World War.

Thanks to his efforts the Royal Navy was not as unready at the beginning of the First World War as it might have been. However one tragedy early on in September 1914, which showed just how much the Navy still had to learn about twentieth-century warfare, involved the former Captain of Osborne, Arthur Christian, now a Rear-Admiral. He was Flag Officer of the 7th Cruiser Squadron stationed off Harwich in the North Sea. In innocence the danger from submarines was not yet properly appreciated and arrangements to ensure a permanent Des-troyer escort were lax. At one point Christian's Flagship *Euryalus* had to return to port to refuel. The Rear-Admiral was prevented by bad weather from transferring his Flag to another ship of the squadron so he had to return to harbour with *Euryalus*, leaving the remaining three cruisers, *Aboukir*, *Hogue* and *Cressy*, in charge of the senior Captain. A U-boat, *U9* spotted them and quickly put a torpedo into *Aboukir*; *Hogue* and *Cressy* stopped at once to pick up survivers, making them-selves sitting targets for more torpedos from *U9* which took immediate advantage of the opportunity. Among the junior officers of the three ships were a large number who had recently left Dartmouth for their final sea training, so it was a particularly heavy blow to that naval generation. In the enquiries that followed Rear-Admiral Christian was exonerated and he retired after more war service in 1919 as Admiral Sir Arthur Christian, dying in 1926.

One person on the naval side who may have had his career permanently blighted by the affair was Lieutenant Burrows. His actions, or rather inaction had been vigorously criticised in court by Carson and this may well have contributed to his failure to make a full naval career; after the First World War he moved into the Colonial Service and took a post in a remote Far Eastern Island Station. Certainly his failure to give any support to a member of his term remains unexplained. It may be that he had formed an unfavourable opinion of George and he would certainly have been aware that the boy's classroom work meant that his days at Osborne could be numbered, but it is at least as probable that he was overawed by Commander Stapleton-Cotton and afraid to stand up to him.

Carson had expounded the responsibilities of a term officer to his charges as he understood them and this was never challenged, but how far a term officer would in practice have been able to oppose the Commander or Captain at this time is problematical. Writing of a slightly later period in his history of Dartmouth* E. A. Hughes says that both term officers and tutors normally "fought like tigers" for their charges' interests but Burrows certainly never did this, and Mr Livesey presumably was given no opportunity to enter into the matter at all. The First World War brought a shake-up which changed attitudes, and future officers at both Osborne and Dartmouth must have noted Carson's strictures.

The First World War caused some disruption in the training of naval officers, and both Osborne and Dartmouth continued in something of a makeshift way, with a pair of retired captains in charge and some of the most experienced of the civilian staff standing in as term officers. The intake was increased greatly and despite the makeshift measures everything on the whole continued smoothly. Allowing some of the civilian staff to take over the responsibilities formerly reserved for the naval side had a permanent benefit as it ended the days when they were kept at arm's length over almost anything not directly concerned with

---

* *The Royal Naval College, Dartmouth:* E. A. Hughes; Winchester Publications 1950.

the classroom, their views on the whole range of college affairs were thereafter always listened to with respect.

Osborne's days were however numbered. Criticisms of the temporary nature of the buildings had increased and also it would clearly be more economic to have everything under one roof. After some more building work a Dartmouth the whole of a cadet's training took place there and the last term left the Isle of Wight in 1921. During Osborne's 18 years 3,967 cadets completed their training there, as well as a few hundred, including George, who for varying reasons failed to complete the course. The buildings themselves were mostly demolished a few years later and their site is today the car park for visitors to Osborne House. The Selbourne scheme survived until after the Second World War when politics intervened and the Labour Government decided it would not tolerate a system designed to cater for entries almost entirely from the class which would otherwise go to public schools. The entry age was raised to 16 and subsequently a variety of 'special entry' arrangements at various levels and ages have been introduced. The Navy today is changing almost as fast as it was when Fisher was shaking it up in Edwardian times, with gunnery replaced by guided rocketry, a complex business requiring considerable technical training.

Commander Stapleton-Cotton also continued on a successful naval career, reaching the rank of Rear-Admiral and retiring in the 1930s. He lived long enough to know of the Rattigan play, and shortly after this was first produced in London in 1946 one of Major Martin's daughters found herself sitting next to a man at a dinner party who turned a very obvious cold shoulder the moment he heard her name. To try and make conversation she enquired if he had seen the play and he replied that he most certainly had not. She then discovered he was the former Commander Stapleton-Cotton who pointedly made it clear that he had neither forgiven nor forgotten before he made an early departure from the party.

While this book was being written, near the end of 1971, there was an almost exact repeat of this incident when one of Major Martin's granddaughters found herself next to a young man at a dinner party who started the evening by ignoring her rather pointedly. Then another member of the party revealed that his father had known George, at which point the young man announced he was Terence Back's son, and that his father had always thought George to be guilty. As young Mr Back was talking to an Archer-Shee his tactlessness received a forceful response; he was picked up by his collar and reminded of the Archer-Shee family motto *Vincit Veritas*, Truth Conquers.

Terence Back had a successful Naval Career, rising to the rank of Captain before retiring just after the Second World War; he died in 1966. His behaviour in this case was always a little ambiguous; there was some uncertainty about his first conversation with CPO Paul and later he certainly denied having any reason to suspect George. In forming an altered conclusion later he differed from most other members of the term, who never doubted George's innocence. A theory grew up among them that the actual culprit was CPO Paul, but there is no evidence to support this belief, which may have been fuelled by a dislike for a man whose duties required him to spend a lot of time chasing them about. On the day in question he was Duty Petty Officer so it would have been impossible for him to leave the college to go to the post office.

The question who did steal the postal order must today remain open. Among officialdom there were many, including Mr McKenna, who always remained convinced George was the thief. It has to be accepted that his innocence was not established beyond all possible doubt, though a close look at the details suggests his guilt is unlikely. A popular theory was that it had all started as a joke, a 'hairy jibe' which had misfired. However neither this, nor the possibility that he took it in a 'sudden moment of temptation' fits in with the clearly established facts. Whoever took the postal order deliberately broke into Back's locker, damaging the lock in the process, so the action was premeditated by at least a few minutes, and a most unlikely move for a practical joker; also if it was a joke then George had an ideal opportunity to explain and make a laugh out of it when he met Back coming out of the reading room on his return from the post office, which was before he had reported to anyone in authority.

Even in the unlikely event that he was the thief, and had stood up to all the pressures on him over so long a period—which would have included visits to confession if his family's Catholic faith meant anything to him at all—then the Admiralty and college authorities still handled the matter with a notable and ill-judged lack of finesse. Had Commander Stapleton-Cotton not allowed his anti-Catholic prejudice to enter in then the investigation could have started more thoroughly and Miss Tucker subjected to less suggestive questions and deeper probing.

It is also clear that once George had left Osborne the Admiralty did not take at all kindly to the decision even being questioned, and only tolerated any further investigations with reluctance. The worst mistake Mr McKenna made was in refusing to allow any representation at Mr Acland's enquiry and so denying Carson a chance to cross-examine Miss Tucker properly at this stage; he compounded this error by the curt letter of refusal which did not even offer the courtesy of any explanation.

The possibility that the offender might be a servant never seems to have entered anyone's head at the college until suggested by Lewis & Lewis; there seems to have been a greater sense of loyalty to the 'old navy men' than to the young charges. Though Major Martin made extensive personal enquiries, and had some suspicions, he unearthed no evidence strong enough to point clearly to anyone else as the culprit; no attempt was made to demolish the accusation against George with a Perry Mason-type denouncement and someone sobbing out a confession in court (which virtually never happens in practice anyway). The coincidence that George was the victim of both mistaken identity and an error by a handwriting expert is made plausible when it is recalled this was exactly the set of circumstances that had recently caused Adolph Beck to serve one five-year term in prison and be convicted a second time before his innocence was established beyond doubt; it was most unfortunate for Beck that he bore a strong resemblance and had similar handwriting to another man who was active in swindling women out of money, and they both lived in the same area.

The significance of the Archer-Shee case can be overrated. Apart from changes in the Osborne regulations it led to no alterations in the law. However such fights as the one waged by the Archer-Shees always have their value for they bring home to authority, both the politicians and the more faceless civil servants, the strength of public feeling about justice and individual rights, which can on occasions become forgotten under the mistaken notion that authority is divine. Afterwards there can be little doubt that the Admiralty and other Government Departments would have been much more careful and ready to listen in similar circumstances.

George was still in the United States finding his feet at Fisk and Robinson when Archduke Ferdinand was assassinated at Sarajevo and Europe slid into the four-year holocaust of the First World War in 1914. This was the time when young men in Britain volunteered in droves to 'do their bit' and the young man who had been turned out of the Navy was no exception. George immediately returned to Britain and enlisted in the Army; he obtained a commission as a Second Lieutenant in the South Staffordshire regiment. From there events took what can now be seen to have been their almost inevitable course. Had he stayed in the Navy his chance of survival through the war would have been fair, particularly as he would have been too old to be among the half-dozen terms which went to sea straight from Dartmouth at the start of the war and who suffered particularly severely in the *Aboukir*, *Hogue* and *Cressy* and other disasters. The odds on a young man enlisting as a subaltern in 1914 living to see 1918 must have been very small indeed, and fate was not prepared to show George any special consideration.

During his short army career he earned some very good opinions; letters after a soldier has been killed in action tend to be fulsome but Colonel Ovens, the officer commanding George's battalion clearly went further than was strictly necessary when he wrote to Mrs Archer-Shee:

> He was a most promising young officer, and in the short time he was in the 1st Battalion, the South Staffordshire Regiment, he earned love and respect of both officers and men, and by his bravery and example contributed largely in the success of the Battalion in the actions near Ypres.

Major Martin also received a personal letter from a brother officer who recalled that George was "such a charming and interesting young fellow, and had seen such a lot of the world for his years, that he was a most pleasant companion at all times and made many friends".

For a while, just what had happened to George was something of a mystery. He was among the British expeditionary force which crossed to France in 1914, the force which Kaiser Wilhelm dubbed a "contemptible little army" but which gave him a number of severe headaches and were never wanting in valour or determination.

During the first Battle of Ypres in the autumn of 1914 George was a platoon commander in the Gheluvelt area. After the battle his name appeared among those listed as missing, which meant he had probably been killed but there was no firm evidence and just a chance he could be a prisoner of war. Britain was starting to learn about the slaughter of the trench warfare all across Europe and only just beginning to become accustomed to long daily casualty lists, which ran into millions before the Armistice, and affected almost every family in the country.

It was a particularly bitter blow for the recently-widowed Mrs Archer-Shee to lose her only son, and the uncertainty of the news only made it worse. She stayed for a while that winter with some friends near Bath, all the time hanging on to a forlorn hope that George might somehow have survived. It was only in the following May that it was finally confirmed he had been killed.

The details that emerged were much to his credit. His platoon had been fighting at an exposed position in the front line in an action which was going badly; the order was sent from HQ for all forces in the area to withdraw, but this failed to reach George. Someone pointed out to him that the units on either side were retiring but he retorted that he did not care what they were doing and told his men that none of them were to retreat until they got the order from him; they continued fighting. Finally the message got through to him and he told his men to get back as best they could. He was the last to leave and later one of his men reported that he had looked round and seen him lying face downward in the earth motionless, still facing the direction of the enemy. The man who made this report was himself killed shortly after, which was one reason why the news penetrated so slowly.

When the story reached the British newspapers it caught their attention and they gave it a prominent place, recalling the fight over his dismissal from Osborne, and observing that despite the treatment he had received he had not hesitated to answer the call to fight for his country. In a special article called "Romance of a Hero" the *Daily Mail* concluded:

> Driven from the Navy by injustice, Lieutenant Archer-Shee has won fame and honour in the Army, and he has served his country well.

His name is inscribed on the Menin Gate at Ypres, on the Stonyhurst War Memorial and on a plaque in the Abbey at Woodchester near Nailsworth. The boy who had been the centrepiece in one of the most unusual legal and political battles in British history died in the way which for young men of his generation was very, very common.

APPENDIX I:
THE PETITION

IN THE HIGH COURT OF JUSTICE.
KING'S BENCH DIVISION

TO THE KING'S MOST EXCELLENT MAJESTY

>THE HUMBLE PETITION OF MARTIN ARCHER-SHEE
>of Nailsworth in the County of Gloucester
>Esquire by his solicitors LEWIS & LEWIS
>of Ely Place Holborn in the County of London.

SHEWETH THAT:—

1. Your Suppliant is the father of George Archer-Shee who was born on the 6th May 1895.
2. At the beginning of the year 1908 it was mutually agreed between Your Suppliant and the Commissioners for executing the office of the Lord High Admiral of the United Kingdom of Great Britain and Ireland (hereinafter called the Admiralty) acting on behalf of Your Majesty that in consideration of Your Suppliant undertaking to make certain annual payments his son should subject to the regulations then in force be admitted into the Royal Naval College at Osborne and there trained as a Naval Cadet with a view to his entering in due course Your Majesty's Navy. The said agreement was made by a written undertaking dated the 1st December 1907 signed by Your Suppliant and

addressed to the Assistant Private Secretary to the First Lord of the Admiralty and a written application (undated) also signed by Your Suppliant and accepted by or on behalf of the Admiralty and the terms thereof were contained partly in the said two documents and partly in the regulations as to entry and examination and the regulations respecting Cadets while at the Royal Naval Colleges at Osborne and Dartmouth published for the information of parents and guardians in the then current number of Your Majesty's Navy List.

3. By the said undertaking Your Suppliant declared and undertook in words following that is to say "I the undersigned being the parent of the candidate to whom the foregoing particulars refer declare that if he obtains a Cadetship it is my intention that he shall adopt the Navy as his profession in life and I heereby undertake to pay the regulated contribution of £75 a year (besides expense of outfit and personal expenses for washing mending clothes and boots pocket money etc.) while my son is in the Royal Naval Training College and to make him a private allowance of £50 a year (besides expenses of outfit) until he reaches the rank of Acting Sub-Lieutenant."

4. Among the said regulations as to entry and examination were the following:—

1. All Naval Cadets enter the service under identical conditions and are trained together until they pass for the rank of lieutenant.

4. Parents or guardians of candidates for appointment as Naval Cadets must undertake for them they they are prepared to serve in any branch if required.

12. For all Cadets entered under these regulations the payment will be at the rate of £75 per annum for the period under training to be paid every term in advance to the Cashier of the Bank of England on receipt of claim from the Accountant-General of the Navy. But the Lords Commissioners of the Admiralty reserve the power of selecting from among the Cadets entered at each examination a limited number being sons of officers of the Navy Army or Marines or of Civil Officers under the Board of Admiralty with respect to whom the annual payment will be £40 only. In this selection their Lordships will have regard solely to the pecuniary circumstances of the Cadet.

Applications for the reduced scale must be received at the Admiralty not later than 1st January 1st May and 1st September.

Parents or Guardians are further required to make a private

allowance of £50 per annum to Cadets from the expiration of their period of training until they reach the rank of Acting Sub-Lieutenant.
13. In addition to the annual payments mentioned in the foregoing paragraph the parent or guardian is charged with the cost of outfit and personal expenses incurred by the Cadet for washing repairing boots and clothes pocket money instruments school books sports etc.
14. The period of training in the College is four years; there are three terms in each year. The first term of each year is approximately from 15th January to 15th April, the second from 7th May to 7th August and the third from 15 September to 15th December.

The vacations are four weeks at Christmas, three weeks at Easter and six weeks at Midsummer.
15. It is to be distinctly understood that the period of training is a time of probation and the parent or guardian of every cadet is required to sign a declaration on the admission of the cadet to the effect that he shall be immediately withdrawn on the receipt of an official request for his withdrawal.

The Lords Commissioners of the Admiralty reserve to themselves full discretion to request the withdrawal of any cadet from the Royal Naval College if after a sufficient trial he is in their opinion for any reason unsuitable for the Naval service. This discretion will as a rule be exercised at the end of the first year but the proficiency and progress of the cadets will be periodically determined and they may be required if necessary to withdraw at a later stage.

16. (A) Reports of progress and conduct are made to the Admiralty at the end of each year of the cadet's study.
   (B) In all subjects of instruction the principle will be followed of giving merit marks for current work. At the end of each year of training the cadet's proficiency and progress is determined partly by examination and partly by the marks gained for current work during the year.
   (C) Cadets who fail to reach a certain standard or who for any reason are considered unsuitable for the Naval Service may be required to withdraw at any time.
      This rule will apply to those who do not show an aptitude for Naval life as well as those who make insufficient progress, or whose constitution is weak although no disease may have developed.

17. Cadets whose conduct is unsatisfactory may at any time be required to withdraw.

18. The parent or guardian of every cadet is required to provide outfit under the regulations in force.

19. No pay is allowed by Government to cadets in the training establishments. The pocket money allowed to cadets is charged to the parents.

Amongst the said regulations respecting cadets while in the Royal Naval College were the following:—

4. The following payment is required from the parents or guardians of each cadet while in the training establishments as a contribution towards the cost of his education:—

At the commencement of each term £25 except in the case of those received at reduced rate of £40 a year whose payments will be £13.16.8. only. Claims will be made upon the parents or guardians by the Accountant-General of the Navy for these sums as they become due and the money should be at once remitted.

19. When a cadet is found to be making insufficient progress a letter is sent to his parent or guardian warning him of the possibility of having to withdraw the cadet unless a marked improvement takes place. This warning is generally issued a term in advance to enable the parent provisionally to make other arrangements for continuing the boy's education in case his withdrawal should become necessary.

5. Your Suppliant's son having duly satisfied the examiners in the qualifying examination and having otherwise fulfilled the requisite preliminaries was accepted by the Admiralty as a Naval Cadet duly admitted for training at the Royal Naval College Osborne in accordance with the above regulations and continued at the College until October 1908. Throughout such time the conduct of Your Suppliant's son was always satisfactory.

6. By letter dated the 17th October 1908 addressed to Your Suppliant the Admiralty purporting to act under the powers conferred upon them by rule 17 of the entry regulations but in fact in breach of the said Agreement required the withdrawal of his said son from the Royal Naval College and Your Suppliant was accordingly compelled against his will to remove his said son from Osborne.

PARTICULARS OF BREACH

The said requisition for withdrawal was by the terms of the said letter expressly based on an allegation that Your Suppliant's son George Archer-Shee was guilty of larceny and forgery videlicet:—That he had stolen a postal order for 5s. and forged the payee's name whereas in truth the said charge was totally devoid of any foundation whatever: the boy was absolutely honest and had had nothing to do with the alleged theft and forgery of the said postal order. The said letter was in the following terms:—

Confidential

N.-11108.   Admiralty

Sir   17th October 1908

I am commanded by my Lords Commissioners of the Admiralty to inform you that they have received a letter from the Commanding Officer of the Royal Naval College at Osborne, reporting the theft of a postal order at the College on the 7th instant which was afterwards cashed at the Post Office.

Investigation of the circumstances of the case leaves no other conclusion possible than that the postal order was taken by your son, Cadet George Archer-Shee.

My Lords deeply regret that they must therefore request you to withdraw your son from the College.

I am, Sir,
Your obedient Servant,
C. I. Thomas

M. Archer-Shee Esq.
Private House,
Bank of England,
Bistol

7. By reason of the premises the good name of Your Suppliant's son has been permanently injured and his prospects in life greatly impaired and the value of the moneys paid by Your Suppliant to the Admiralty pursuant to the said Agreement has been lost to him.

Your Suppliant therefore humbly prays that Your Majesty will be pleased to declare:—

1. That George Archer-Shee had not stolen the said Postal Order or forged the payee's name and was innocent of the charge made

against him by the Admiralty in the said letter of the 17th October 1908.

2. That the requisition of the Admiralty to Your Suppliant to withdraw his son from the Royal Naval College was a breach of the Agreement between Your Suppliant and the Admiralty.

And that Your Majesty will be further pleased to do what is right and just in the premises and cause Your Suppliant to be reimbursed and compensated for the damages so sustained by him as aforesaid.

And Your Suppliant prays that Your Majesty may be graciously pleased to direct this Petition to be indorsed with Your Majesty's fiat "Let right be done".

Dated the 18th day of May, 1909.

EDWARD CARSON.

LESLIE SCOTT.

APPENDIX II:

THE TELLING OF THE STORY: SOURCES AND SELECT BIBLIOGRAPHY

The first occasion I can discover that the story was 'written up' was by Mr Edward Majoriebanks in 1932. Mr Marjoriebanks made his name with a biography of Sir Edward Marshall Hall and was then invited to write an 'official' life of Carson. He was at work on this with close co-operation from Carson and his family, and he had completed his work up to the chapter which covered the Archer-Shee case when he killed himself in a sudden fit of depression. The chapter he left is valuable because he had discussed the matter with Carson, but contains a few errors in detail. This biography was finished by the late Ian Colvin and published by Gollancz.

Shortly after this, another young lawyer-writer, Derek Walker-Smith (now Sir Derek), included a valuable essay on legal aspects of the case in his *Lord Reading and his Cases*, 1934, Chapman and Hall.

The first 'popular' account was the essay by the American writer and personality Alexander Woollcott (the original 'Man who Came to Dinner'), who had the idea suggested to him by President Franklin Roosevelt, a friend of the Archer-Shee family. This first appeared in *The Atlantic Monthly* in 1939 and has been republished on a number of occasions, first in Britain in *Long, Long Ago*, a collection of Woollcott writings published by Cassell & Co in 1945.

Lord Reading covered the matter briefly and fairly in his biography of his father published by Hutchinson & Co in 1942.

In *Carson: Lord Carson of Duncairn*, Heinemann 1953, H. Montgomery Hyde produced an authorative biography which set the record straight on a number of Mr Marjoriebanks's errors.

Sir Terence Rattigan's play *The Winslow Boy* was first produced in London at the Lyric Theatre in 1946. It won the Ellen Terry Award there and when presented in New York in 1947 won the Critics' Prize. A subsequent film was also very successful, and the play was revived in London in 1970.

The true story has been broadcast by the BBC on a number of occasions, told by both Edgar Lustgarten and Vincent Broome, and also appears in various anthologies of interesting legal cases.

Of unpublished sources the most substantial and significant are in the Public Record Office, file ADM 116/1085a which supplied most of the material in this book not attributed elsewhere. It includes all the internal Admiralty papers on the case, various statements taken from witnesses, the reports by both Lord Desart and Mr Acland, and a full transcript of the trials. The Post Office also have a substantial file, though much of this deals with routine matters about making arrangements for witnesses it does include the postal orders. Other documents are among the McKenna papers at Churchill College Cambridge which I was allowed to see by courtesy of Mr David McKenna, at Stonyhurst College and with the Archer-Shee family.

During my researches the *Daily Telegraph* published an appeal for personal recollections which resulted in a substantial number of letters reaching me, the most important writers are named in the Preface.

Other books and publications which have played their part in building this story are:

The Royal Naval College, Dartmouth, E. A. Hughes, Winchester Publications, 1950
The Wind of Morning, Colonel Sir Hugh Bousted, Chatto & Windus, 1971
From the Dreadnought to Scapa Flow, Arthur J. Marder, Oxford University Press, 1960
Suspect Documents: Their Scientific Examination, Wilson R. Harrison, Sweet & Maxwell, 1958

Charlie B: the Life of Lord Charles Beresford, Geoffrey Bennett, Peter Dawnay, 1968
The Strange Death of Liberal England, George Dangerfield, 1935
The Osborne Magazine
The Stonyhurst College Magazine and War Record
The Dictionary of National Biography
Hansard

Contemporary reports and comments, in particular in:

The Times
Daily Telegraph
Morning Post
Daily Mirror
The Nation

INDEX

Titles and Ranks of those directly involved in the story are those applicable at the time; some of them, the naval officers in particular, later rose to higher positions. Italics denote an illustration and an asterisk★ that the reference is only in a footnote.

RMB

185